LEADERSHIP
FRONT AND CENTER

A DECADE OF
THOUGHT AND TUTELAGE

ERVIN (EARL) COBB
Leadership Development Consultant and Bestselling Author

OTHER BOOKS BY
Ervin (Earl) Cobb

The SMART Leader and the Skinny Principles
How to Lead and Win within Any Organization

Driving Ultimate Project Performance
Transforming from Project Manager to Project Leader

The Official Leadership Checklist and Diary
for Project Management Professionals

The Leadership Advantage
Do More. Lead More. Earn More.

God's Goodness & Our Mindfulness
Responding versus Reacting to Life Changing Circumstances

Focused Leadership
What You Can Do Today to Become a More Effective Leader

Pillow Talk Consciousness
Intimate Reflections on America's 100 Most Interesting
Thoughts and Suspicions

Navigating the Life Enrichment Model™

Living a Richer Life
Getting the Most out of Life's Gifts and Circumstances

Copyright © 2020 by Ervin Cobb

Published by RICHER Press
An Imprint of Richer Life, LLC
5710 Ogeechee Road, Suite 200-175, Savannah, Georgia 31405
www.richerlifellc.com

Cover Design: RICHER Media USA
Photographs: Bigstock Photo®

Volume book discounts are available for groups, companies, and organizations. Contact the publisher for information and order instructions.

No part of this publication may be reproduced, stored in a retrieval system, or transmitted in any form or by any means, electronic, mechanical, photocopying, recording, scanning, or otherwise, except as permitted under Section 107 or 108 of the 1976 United States Copyright Act, without prior written permission of the publisher.

LEADERSHIP FRONT AND CENTER
A Decade of Thoughts and Tutelage

Ervin (Earl) Cobb a
p. cm.

1. Leadership   2. Management   3. Self-Improvement
(pbk : alk. Paper)

Library of Congress Control Number: 2020942267

ISBN-13: 978-1-7335693-2-3

PRINTED IN THE UNITED STATES OF AMERICA

September 2020

Ervin (Earl) Cobb
PRAISE FOR HIS WORK

"Mr. Cobb has been meticulously working on advancing what is known in the realm of Leadership Development. He is a proven author of several books, a well-known speaker, a leader, and has a genius approach to leadership development. The information that he provides in his latest body of work is "textbook worthy" and I highly recommend all colleges/universities/companies adopt this body of work to teach Leadership Development"

— **Jonathan Hebert, M. Eng, PMP, Ph.D., Program Manager/Raytheon, Owner/Randy Brevard Holdings**

"The Cobbs have written a leadership book that is easy to read with practical, apply it right now, techniques. This book is chock full of tips, techniques, and best practices in leadership that will be of value to new leaders of any generation. Their "Skinny" Principles, shared in each chapter, will undoubtedly be earmarked, and highlighted by readers and referred to regularly. This book is a MUST READ for new leaders. Plus, leaders who have been in their role for a while will likely also find a nugget or two to take away and apply."

— **Gina Abudi, MBA, President, Abudi Consulting Group, LLC, Author** of *Implementing Positive Organizational Change: A Strategic Project Management Approach*, J Ross Publishing, 2017

"The book is EXCEPTIONAL & definitely a must read!!!! The principles are helping me transition from "managing" my team at my organization to "leading" my team."

— **Glori Allen, BlueCross BlueShield of South Carolina Information Systems Training Manager.**

ACKNOWLEDGEMENTS

I would like to acknowledge the over 11,000 LinkedIn network connections and faithful Social Media followers.

A special thanks to the thousands of you who have read and commented on my published articles over the past decade. The hundreds of messages and thousands of "likes" have increased my energy and dedication for doing what I do.

CONTENTS

INTRODUCTION 11

PUBLISHED ARTICLES

1. MY CASE FOR WHY IT/BUSINESS MISALIGNMENT IS AN IT LEADERSHIP ISSUE — 15
2. YOUR BEST LIFE COULD BE AHEAD OF YOU: JUST REMEMBER, "WHAT YOU KNOW" — 27
3. AS A LEADER, YOUR SILENCE SPEAKS LOUDER THAN ANY OF YOUR MESSAGES — 31
4. ELON MUSK AND THE FALCON 9 ROCKET SHIP LEADS WITH INTENTION — 35
5. THIS IS WHAT MAKES MY DAYS MOST MEMORABLE. WHAT ABOUT YOURS? — 41
6. HOW TO LEAD WITH INTENTION AND NOT AUTHORITY — 45
7. A KEY POST COVID-19 LEADERSHIP LESSON: THINGS CHANGE – BUT NOT HUMANITY — 47
8. BEING PRESENT WHEN DECISIONS ARE BEING MADE DURING "UNCERTAIN" TIMES — 51
9. ORGANIZATIONAL LEADERSHIP IN A POST COVID 19 WORLD - A NEED FOR EVERYONE TO STEP UP THEIR GAME — 57
10. WHY LEADERSHIP DURING A CRISIS LIKE THE CORONAVIRUS DEMANDS EMPATHY — 71
11. MANAGING CHANGE REQUIRES A NEW PLAYBOOK FOR SUCCESS — 75
12. THE NATURAL PROGRESSION TO MASTERING LEADERSHIP SKILLS — 79
13. HIGH-PERFORMERS - YOU CAN'T PARK THERE — 83
14. RESOLVE TO BETTER MANAGE CONFLICT WITHIN YOUR ORGANIZATION AND YOUR LIFE — 87
15. FOUR OF MY BIGGEST LESSONS LEARNED IN 2019 — 89
16. HOW PREPARED ARE YOU TO PROTECT YOURSELF AND DO YOUR JOB TODAY? — 93

CONTENTS

PUBLISHED ARTICLES

17. SKINNY PRINCIPAL #1 – IT DOES MATTER — 97
18. WHAT IS THE MOST IMPORTANT "C" WITHIN YOUR ORGANIZATION — 99
19. THE GREAT MYSTERY AWAITS US ALL — 103
20. LEADERSHIP IS SO MISUNDERSTOOD — 105
21. WHY LIVING A RICHER LIFE IS LESS MYSTERY AND MORE MASTERY — 107
22. IS NARRATIVE ENHANCED LEADERSHIP WHAT YOU HAVE BEEN LOOKING FOR? — 111
23. THE NEED TO ELEVATE YOUR GAME IN ORDER TO MOVE TO AND SUCCEED AT THE NEXT LEVEL — 113
24. THE MOTHER OF ALL HOLIDAY WISHES — 115
25. BELIEVE IT OR NOT – THIS IS WHY PROJECT MANAGERS ARE BECOMING LEADERS — 117
26. WHY MORE PROJECT MANAGERS ARE BECOMING PROJECT LEADERS — 119
27. WHEN THEY FEEL YOUR PRESENCE IN YOUR ABSENCE - YOU HAVE LED — 123
28. A PROFESSIONAL AND PERSONAL ADVANTAGE YOU MIGHT BE MISSING AND WHAT YOU ARE LOSING — 127
29. WHY TRADITIONAL LEADERSHIP TRAINING ROUTINELY FAIL PROJECT LEADERS – PART ONE — 129
30. WHY TRADITIONAL LEADERSHIP TRAINING ROUTINELY FAIL PROJECT LEADERS – PART TWO — 133
31. WHY THINKING LIKE A LEADER IS MORE THAN HALF THE BATTLE — 139

ABOUT THE AUTHOR — 145

INTRODUCTION

A DECADE OF THOUGHTS AND TUTELAGE

As I stated in my book, *"The Leadership Advantage: Do More. Lead More. Earn More"*:

Without question, leadership is one of the most studied, documented, discussed, celebrated and sometimes mystifying subjects that mankind has encountered. This apparent confusion and/or transformation of leadership theories has been going on for centuries, as revealed in the philosophical writings from Plato's Republic. Yet still, none of us can escape the fact that we spend most of our lives either leading or being led.

Yes. Believe it or not, leadership in some form or fashion is omnipresent within all of today's societies, institutions, and organizations. The study and discussion of leaders and the discipline of leadership is an enduring effort by many – including yours truly.

If you are a student of contemporary leadership development and training, I am sure that you are familiar with some of the approaches and discussions surrounding the guidance, teaching and training of organizational leaders and how to best help them develop effective leadership skills. Here are just a few:

- There are discussions about *"Leading from the Front"* or by example. This approach proposes that managers develop skills which allow them to demonstrate their leadership by going first. In many cases, this is accomplished by managers doing the tough things first to show that they can be done.

- There are conversations around *"Leading from the Middle."* The advocates here suggest that this approach helps to bring out the best in others, so that associates can realize and step into their own potential to create needed change.

- There is the approach of *"Leading from the Center."* The enthusiasts here recommend that leaders in middle management roles acquire skills that support their ability to be cognizant of the perspectives of both those they are leading as well as those leading them; and

- With *Technology Development and Deployment Projects* playing an increasing role in how business strategy is executed within 21st century organizations, *"Project Leadership"* has evolved as a unique leadership discipline. This team-based leadership discipline has aroused rapidly increasing global interest. However, formal training and development opportunities addressing the differences between Project Management vs. Project Leadership are slow to evolve.

Buried deep within all the suggestions and discussions are the demanding and sometimes frustrating challenges faced by most managers attempting to determine which approach best fits their current needs - given their career stage and their actual role within the organization.

After decades of *leading and being led* within Fortune 100, Mid-Market, and Venture companies, it became apparent to me that it was *generally assumed* that employees hired to be *managers* within organizations come aboard equipped with the organizational leadership skills required to also function as *effective leaders*.

Of course, nothing was or is further from the truth.

Management change after *management change* and *performance failure* after *performance failure* has revealed the fact that becoming an effective leader within any organization requires a specific, clear, and thoughtful leadership development plan. It also requires individualized and targeted leadership training.

So, a decade ago, after retiring from a thirty-four-year career in corporate America and becoming a leadership consultant, I decided that all my work would be centered around what I now call, a *Triangular Approach* to leadership development success.

A *Triangular Approach* closely examines three *essential factors* that must be evaluated, understood, and considered in the determination of a manager's leadership development needs.

This thorough and candid examination is vital to a process which ensures the development of a clear path to leadership success.

These essential factors include the *specific leadership challenge*, the *inherent individual traits,* and the *organizational culture.*

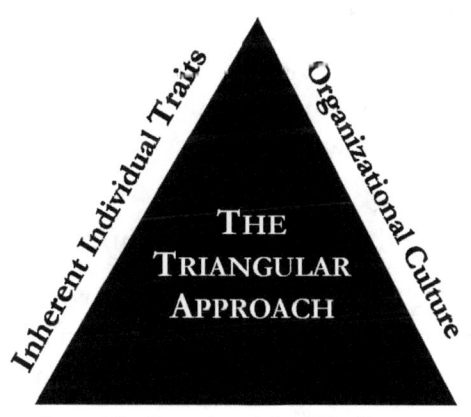

Over the years, by evaluating, understanding, and considering all three of these essential factors during my engagements, I have discovered how the best aspects of relevant contemporary leadership development approaches can be incorporated more effectively into my training, coaching and published work.

I believe that this *Triangular Approach* not only ensures a more realistic path for a manager's leadership development success but also creates the best opportunity for organizational success.

Based on the tremendous feedback I have received regarding the thoughts, messages and teachings included in the collection of articles in this book, I do believe that I have made a difference in the careers of many managers and readers over the past decade.

The thirty-one articles cover a range of topics and have varying levels of detail and leadership focus. However, they all are anchored in respected contemporary leadership studies, proven research, and my personal experiences.

If asked to describe the nature of this collection of articles, I would have to use the phrase, *Leadership Front and Center*.

My use of the phrase *Leadership Front and Center* implies that there are two critical *positions* where all managers should always find themselves - to function as effective leaders and to maintain the leadership presence they desire.

The first is to always be in "front" of both their personal and professional developmental needs as well as the needs and expectations of the organization they are leading.

The second is to always be at the "center" of all the actions necessary for both them and their organization to be successful.

It is my hope that within each article you will gain some new insights and maybe find a "nugget" that will provide a spark to your quest to becoming a more effective organizational leader.

If you do, then my decade of documenting and sharing my thoughts on leadership development and passionately providing tutelage to managers and readers will mean that much more.

LEADERSHIP FRONT AND CENTER

MY CASE FOR WHY IT/BUSINESS MISALIGNMENT IS AN IT LEADERSHIP ISSUE

Published on July 23, 2020

Yes. Every IT and Business Team Member impacts his or her organization's performance and success. They all desire to do a great job and contribute to overall business success - even though at times - internal activities, performance and outcomes are "misaligned."

However, your role as the Information Technology (IT) organization's leader has by far the largest and most direct effect on IT organizational culture, cohesiveness, and performance. All three of which are paramount in efforts  to eliminate IT/Business misalignment. The IT leadership role involves much more than the accurate translation of business requirements into technical requirements.

It also demands that you, as the IT leader, to have an adequate level of "leadership presence" during all phases of development, implementation and post-implementation — to eliminate potential issues, fix problematic releases and drive home "lessons learned" to prevent future mishaps and misalignment.

In today's leadership training, the expression "leadership presence" focuses on a manager's ability to assume a leadership role "throughout" the organization and to communicate, with confidence, the business strategy. In this case, it includes clearly articulating the IT role in helping to successfully execute the strategy. The goal is always to ensure that all IT Team Members understand that the IT department's "primary role — is to "enable" the technology portion of the business strategy and to support the end user's needs.

If what IT is being asked "to do" presents significant challenges, requires additional resources or may be technically or structurally not possible, it is your role — as the IT organization's leader — to quickly address these issues with senior management. You should not lead your organization down a "loser's path."

When IT Leadership "fails" to ensure that all its daily communications and reinforcement in this regard are both clear and persuasive — the resulting IT/Business misalignment — is an IT leadership issue.

As the leader, not being physically, mentally, and emotionally "present" when it comes to the allocation of resources, the management of major risks and the validation of the corporate strategy is equivalent to you being seriously "missing in action". Without exception, you must always be "present with your presence" in order to ensure that you — and your IT organization — are in the best position possible to perform your role as a critical "enabler" of organizational success in today's highly technology-driven business environment.

Here is a short story, which will help to illuminate my case.

The story is fictional, however the actual findings of the protagonist are consistent with my professional experience during my tenures as Corporate VP of Enterprise Process Development with the Reynolds and Reynolds Company and as the Technology Area Manager and Head of Data Center Management for the Wells Fargo Bank.

You will find the story at the end of this article. Go there now and enjoy the rest of a suspenseful and insightful read.

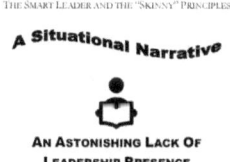

As concluded by AJ, the protagonist in this narrative, "Without such presence, it is nearly impossible to develop a winning level of organizational cohesiveness, gain concurrence among your work teams on [business] strategy and create the organizational momentum required to win [i.e. stay aligned with business and customer needs].

This does not mean that it is your job, as the IT organization's leader, to "do all the work."

However, it is your job and your responsibility to collaborate with your Team Leads strategically, tactically and operationally to ensure that the entire IT organization is in full alignment with the current business plan and strategy on all major projects and internal/external service agreements within its IT portfolio.

My decades of experience as both a business executive and a technology development leader indicate that, unknowingly, many IT leaders have fundamental shortcomings in this area. Too often, they fail to understand or accept their full responsibility for ensuring that the required leadership for business alignment is "present" throughout the organization.

They unconsciously fail to do some or all the following:

1. They fail to clearly articulate their leadership expectations for "business alignment" within all three levels of the IT organization's leadership structure — strategic, tactical, and operational.

2. They fail to adapt their personal involvement to the level required to meet the leadership needs of each project team and unique business requests.

3. They fail to take the time to understand, appraise and provide constructive feedback regarding the performance of their Team Leads in all "tactical" and "operational" roles.

4. They fail to create the work environment and the internal processes required to make it "non-threatening" for their Team Leads to seek their input and involvement regarding potential business misalignment issues and challenges.

5. They fail to create a culture that broadens the opportunity for all Team Members to develop the leadership skills required to understand and accurately compare and map IT requirements/processes to business requirements and, more importantly, anticipated outcomes; and

6. They fail to identify, investigate, and make the decisions required to remove internal performance roadblocks, which typically result in business misalignment.

I believe that by taking the following steps, you can adequately address these fundamental shortcomings.

STEP 1: Review the six shortcomings listed above. Determine how many of these shortcomings you need to address and what you will do to address them.

STEP 2: If your organization is less than 50 team members, you should meet individually with all your "team leads". Here is a process you can use:

   a. Share with them the type of work relationship and environment that you envision regarding your level of involvement in the organization's tactical and operational leadership levels — particularly around how the technical road map aligns with business requirements and expectations.

   b. Then, ask for their thoughts and opinions.

   c. If there is a mutual and honest consensus that such a work relationship and environment already exist, you are good.

d. If there is not such a consensus, ask for input on what he or she believes would be the best path to arrive at this type of work relationship and environment.

   e. Develop a plan and implement it. The follow-up here can be included in future performance reviews.

STEP 3: If your organization is larger than 50 team members, you should meet individually with all your "direct reports" and have a similar discussion as described in STEP 2. Then, request that all your direct reports have and document similar discussions with their direct reports who are Team Leads.

Remember — Leadership is not something you just think about — Leadership is something you do.

A Situational Narrative

An Astonishing Lack Of Leadership Presence

My flight arrived in Charlotte, North Carolina at eleven o'clock Thursday night. The flight from Phoenix was over four hours long and fortunately, it was without any delays. It was after midnight by the time I collected my bag, caught a cab and checked into my downtown hotel room.

My wife and I lived in the Charlotte area for about seven years in the early 2000s. I was quite familiar with Charlotte's downtown development history and was eager to see what had changed over the past decade. However, there will not be any time this trip for a tour of the Queen City.

This is an unscheduled and unusual business trip and mission for me. This business trip only permits me to spend twenty-four hours here in Charlotte. My mission is to conduct a corporate investigation and to prepare a confidential report this weekend in support of a Monday morning deliverable commitment I made to a special client earlier this week.

My first meeting will start at seven in the morning and I will most likely not complete all of my meetings and interviews until late in the evening. Why am I here, you ask? First, let me take the time to share with you a little background on myself and some basic, but important, insights into the disturbing, yet often repeated, organizational performance challenge I have been asked to investigate.

****

My name is Anthony Jerome McAdoo. Most people call me AJ.

I retired from my 30-year career in corporate America around ten years ago. My last corporate position was as a Senior Technology Manager and the Head of Data Center Management for the Capital Cargo Bank.

On Monday of this week, I attended an Executive Leadership Conference in San Francisco. While there, I met Ralph Dean, the new President and CEO of the Capital Cargo Bank. He moved into this role after I had left Capital Cargo in 2009. During a lunch conversation, I shared with Ralph a few highlights of my tenure with Capital Cargo. I also mentioned the fact that I was attending this particular Leadership Conference because I am now a leadership development consultant with a keen interest in helping organizational leaders understand the true power of leadership.

I was somewhat surprised when Ralph asked if I could meet him for dinner that same evening. He wanted to discuss a somewhat mystifying organizational and business performance challenge he and the Capital Cargo executive team were currently facing. Not satisfied with the feedback he was receiving from a consultant he hired a few months ago, he indicated that he was interested in getting another perspective on the challenge. I said, *"Sure. It would be my pleasure."*

I met Ralph for dinner that evening around eight-thirty. I must admit that I was a little shocked with his degree of candor. I learned that he was very concerned about a presentation he had to give to Capital Cargo Bank's Board of Directors in a meeting scheduled for next week.

It turns out that Capital Cargo has experienced multiple outages of their online banking system over the past six months. All of the outages were traced back to a critical Data Center located in Charlotte, North Carolina. The daylong outages were having a severely negative impact on Capital Cargo's customer base and stock price. Any additional outages simply could not be tolerated.

Surprisingly, after several weeks of working with a consultant who was dispatched to Charlotte to determine the root cause of the problem, Ralph's executive team still could not provide him an explanation of the problem that he felt was adequate. In his words, *"The explanations I have been given to this point simply don't hold water; and can't be presented to my Board of Directors next Tuesday."*

After providing an hour-long breakdown of the situation and the most recent findings, Ralph asked if I could take a trip to the Charlotte Data Center and spend a day with the Data Center senior management team. He also asked if I would provide him a report detailing what I thought was the root cause of the problems and what might be a possible solution. He needed the report the following Monday.

Having a technical background, Ralph was less concerned with the feedback he had received regarding the technical issues and more concerned with what he perceived as a *lack of senior leadership focus and organizational cohesiveness.*

Sensing that Ralph was sincerely interested in getting my perspective and that he would give my report a fair hearing, I agreed to modify my schedule to include a trip to Charlotte later in the week. The plan will be to learn about the root cause of Capital Cargo's problems and determine a possible solution.

****

Thus, here I am in Charlotte. As I mentioned earlier, tomorrow I will meet with the Charlotte Data Center senior management team. I also plan to meet with and interview as many of the other members of the Charlotte work team as possible. My goal is to gain some operative insight into what is really going at Capital Cargo's Charlotte Center, both operationally and organizationally. I intend to provide a report to Ralph Dean on Monday morning.

****

Well, it's Saturday morning and I am back in my office in Phoenix working to complete the report I will deliver to Ralph Dean and Capital Cargo Monday morning. For about three hours now, I have been reviewing notes from my meetings and interviews. During my twenty-plus hours in Charlotte, I met with the entire Capital Cargo Data Center senior management team and interviewed all of the key members of the technical and project staff.

In summary, about half of what I discovered and observed was not surprising. However, the other half was quite disturbing.

First, here is the half that was not surprising.

> The consolidation of four older regional data centers into the new Charlotte Data Center concluded about six months ago. Prior to this consolidation effort, Capital Cargo had not experienced a daylong outage of their online banking system in over 10 years.

> When I arrived at the Charlotte Data Center Friday morning, the first thing I discovered was that, since the consolidation project's completion, most of the Charlotte team has been working through numerous problems with the installation of new server technology, the upgrade of old technology and a massive data migration effort. All of this was in addition to the normal activity associated with data center operations.

> Because of the magnitude of the consolidation effort and the new skill-sets required to integrate the disparate systems, the project required a significant amount of leadership presence to sort through the available skills and competences of the Data Center's technical and project staff.

> Based on my experience, I knew that the key to any successful consolidation effort of this type is to have a comprehensive integration strategy and work plan at all levels of the organization.

Not surprising, throughout the data center facility, I found a dedicated and committed technical and project staff. They were working long hours and overtime was abundant. I have learned over the years that this situation frequently occurs at the end of most large system integration and data migration projects. Therefore, these initial findings were not a surprise.

However, it soon became apparent to me that the team's major challenges were three-fold: 1) the lack of a comprehensive problem resolution strategy; 2) the lack of an organizational-wide work plan; and 3) the lack of an adequate level of leadership presence. For me to discover major gaps in *strategic, tactical and operational leadership* — months after system "go live" — was quite unusual. The absence of attention and presence at all three of these levels of leadership in a corporation the size of Capital Cargo was unthinkable.

Now, here is the other half of what I discovered and observed at the Charlotte Data Center. This is the part that astonishingly, left me both surprised and quite disturbed.

Although the Capital Cargo Data Center senior management team included experienced technologist and managers, it was apparent during my visit that this particular team lacked the senior leadership skills required to lead such a complex and multi-facetted consolidation. The turnover rate of both the project management and technical staff had increased significantly over the last few months. After only a few hours at the Center, I could sense a general feeling of desperation at all levels of the organization.

A couple of senior team leads shared with me during private interviews that, starting a few months ago, the sense of desperation seemed to have increased sharply. This was about the same time that most members of the middle management team began to feel that they *had to* and were *expected to* spend most of their time on the operations floor to help "do the work".

During my discussions with the team's project managers, I discovered that a few members of the senior management team did stay in the position to recognize global integration issues surrounding the consolidation project. They also had the authority to quickly shift or add the skills and resources required to more proactively resolve issues. However, after multiple requests by several project managers, they failed to do so.

In conclusion, it became clear to me that there was simply not a sufficient level of senior leadership presence in the Charlotte Data Center organization. Without such presence, it was nearly impossible to develop a winning level of cohesiveness, gain concurrence on an overall resolution strategy and create the organizational momentum required for the Charlotte Center to be successful — and outage free.

****

On Monday morning, I submitted what I believe was an honest and very comprehensive report to Ralph Dean and Capital Cargo's executive team, as promised.

The cover page of my report included:

Report on the Charlotte Data Center Performance Challenge

Root Cause: Senior Leadership Missing in Action

Solution: Leadership Training and/or New Leaders Needed

****

A few weeks later, while heading home from work, I received the following text message from Ralph Dean:

"Thanks, AJ. Good job. Just as I suspected. An astonishing lack of leadership presence. It was an extremely difficult Board meeting last month. New leadership team now in place at the Charlotte Data Center. Corporate-wide leadership training sessions will start soon."

Your Best Life Could be Ahead of You: Just Remember, "What You Know"

Published on June 21, 2020

This article is not about me. It's about you.

When I left the Wells Fargo Bank in 2010 and left behind a 34 year corporate career with some of the best companies of my era, I had no idea what my life would be like ten years down the road.

I must admit that after thirty-four years of learning and contributing at all levels within organizations of various types and sizes, there was some doubt about what I wanted to do next.

However, one thing was without any reservation, "I knew what I knew".

What I knew was – *where I had been, what I had learned, what I liked, what I didn't like, what I didn't want to do anymore* and *what I wanted to be able to continue doing*.

Little did I know that ten years down the road, much of what would become my true life's legacy would not be grounded in my past...but framed by my future.

Surprisingly, this legacy would not be driven as much by the "companies" where I spent more than half of my life…but by the "company", I would be fortunate enough to keep and bring into my life over the past ten years.

My kind of "company" included energetic editors, patient publishers, candid critics, faithful friends, and a wonderful wife.

They all unconditionally supported my life-long desire to research, write and publish books and articles about the power of *leadership* and *human thought* – which, as evidenced by book sales and personal feedback, have shaped other's thoughts and changed many lives for the better.

However, as I mentioned earlier, this article is not about me. It's about you.

I just felt that I had to *paint the above picture* of some professional credibility and personal conquest  before I share with you an important fact that you should keep top-of-mind during this period. That is… your best life could be ahead of you.

During these times, as we all attempt to work our way through this global medical pandemic and this amazingly historic moment in American history, it is only human for uncertainty, isolation, and disruption to create some doubt about what our future will look like – especially those of you who are in the middle or at the peak of rewarding careers.

Regardless of where you are today in your career [*feeling okay, treading water, stalled, challenged or derailed*], I would like to offer, hopefully, just another voice to remind you that – your best life could be ahead of you.

My experience, research and observations remind me that it is important for you to do two things:

- First, take this moment to sit down, write down and internalize *what you know, where you have been, what you have learned, what you liked, what you didn't like, what you don't want to do anymore* and *what you want to be able to continue doing*; and

- Secondly, think seriously about the "company" you currently have in your life (*both personally and professionally*) and determine who and what is missing…and what else is needed to actualize and maximize what your future could hold. Then, do what must be done to close the gap.

Yes, your best life could be ahead of you.

Just, always remember, the only thing standing between *could* and *will* and the future legacy you desire is *you*.

"Over the past decade, I have spent much of my time researching, interviewing, and writing about organizational leaders."

As a Leader, Your Silence Speaks Louder Than Any of Your Messages

Published on June 21, 2020

During my 34-year corporate career, I have worked for dozens of good managers in Fortune 100, Mid-Market, and venture companies. I worked hard for all of them and did everything I could do to meet all their expectations, as an employee.

Some of my managers were good organizational leaders. Some others I would not consider leaders at all and I can barely remember their names.

There were a few managers who I once thought were good leaders. But, over time, they managed to lose my trust. For some reason, I can vividly remember their names...but not much else they ever said.

Over the past decade, I have spent much of my time researching, interviewing, and writing about organizational leaders. My primary focus in all of my leadership development work has been a desire to gain a sense of not just a leader's personal and professional attributes, but also their true character *(the mental and moral qualities distinctive to an individual)* and how they, when not guarded, *really saw the world* around them.

Based on my research, observation, and personal experiences, I have learned three things that might come as a surprise to many managers who have organizational leadership responsibilities.

1. You cannot manage your way out of circumstances that require specific leadership skills. Skills such as:

    - *Actively listening* to gain a deeper understanding of a new idea, a risky approach or unusual circumstance.

    - Intentionally broadening your perspective of unfamiliar places or people to block out the typical *"fight or flight"* responses that everyone unconsciously receives *(from the wizards we call our brains)* when confronted with something new; and

    - Increasing your *powers of reassurance* by gaining important insights about others – insights that can only be gained by being a truly empathetic leader.

2. You must be totally convinced that it is your responsibility to both manage and lead your organization with a clear understanding that *managing* and *leading* are both required. Also, knowing that to be effective, each distinctive approach to *managing* vs *leading* is instantly recognizable by the people who work for you.

3. If you suddenly find yourself confronted with an issue, which cuts to the core of your character *(i.e. who you really are or what is really in your heart)*, the worst thing you can do, as a leader, is to be silent. From an employee's perspective, your *silence* is the loudest message you can send.

A leader's silence on issues of broad importance is equivalent to purchasing a neon billboard and publicly confessing the hidden thoughts you care not to reveal. Even when equipped with the training and development required to become an effective leader, leadership acumen cannot hide true character.

As a leader, you are expected to clearly express your position on issues of company and cultural importance.

Being silent, even for the shortest period, can lead to losing the trust of those you are leading – leading them to vividly remember your name – and not much else you have ever said.

"Take a break from today's headlines and enjoy a little 20th century American history on learning to lead."

LEADERSHIP FRONT AND CENTER

ELON MUSK AND THE FALCON 9 ROCKET SHIP
LEADS WITH INTENTION

Published on May 30, 2020

Elon Musk and SpaceX made history today. Musk's commercially built Falcon 9 rocket ship thundered away from Earth with two Americans aboard. An American achievement not seen since NASA retired the space shuttle in 2011. It was quite a leadership feat.

National leadership is what many American's are seriously thinking about these days.

It's what I have being thinking and writing about for decades. It appears that today, the need to be authoritarian, loud, controlling and "right" is dominating the airways and byways. While --- as we all know --- "right" is one of the most "relative" words in the English language.

Well, from leading scores of teams and projects over the past thirty years and having experimented with various leadership styles, I have come to believe that *leading with intention*, versus depending on your authority, gets far better results. I believe that most people who really understand what effective leadership is about would agree.

Leading with intention means establishing a clear vision of where you are taking your team and creating an effective method to communicate that vision both "upward" and "downward."

Here's an anecdote from my first book on Leadership Development titled *"Focused Leadership: What You Can Do Today to Become a More Effective Leader"* – which just happen to be published in 2011.

Take a break from today's headlines and enjoy a little 20th Century American history on *learning to lead.*

FIRST CLASSIFIED DOD SPACE SHUTTLE MISSION

At 4:23 p.m. EST on January 27, 1985 the Space Shuttle Discovery appeared to touch down without a hitch at the Kennedy Space Center in Florida after successfully completing its mission and traveling a total of 1.3 million miles.

None of the tens of thousands observing the magnificent landing of this spaceship were aware that during the planned external tank separation, the backup flight system (BFS) did not automatically proceed to the proper landing mode. The crew of five astronauts, including the Commander, Thomas Mattingly, and Pilot Loren Shriver, had to quickly react and perform the necessary manual procedures to resume normal landing operations. The BFS operated satisfactorily until the Shuttle's final deorbit maneuver.

For some reason, the BFS deorbit maneuver ignition was 8 seconds late. Fortunately, the BFS miraculously operated satisfactorily from that point for a safe touch down and landing.

There were many other significant behind the scene maneuvers that contributed to the successful mission of what was called STS-51-C. However, without one much larger behind the scene maneuver that started several years earlier, STS-51-C's mission would not have been possible.

This mission critical maneuver involved a well-coordinated and massive effort to retrofit the Space Shuttle with a special capability required for STS-51-C to accomplish its sensitive mission. This complicated project would eventually consist of hundreds of trained professionals, millions of contract-related dollars, a magnificent technology deployment and a remarkable leadership feat.

STS-51-C was the first classified Department of Defense (DoD) mission of the Space Shuttle. The U.S. National Aeronautics and Space Administration (NASA) Space Transportation System (STS) vehicle was rolled out in 1981. The STS, more commonly known as the Space Shuttle, was the first operational orbital spacecraft designed for reuse.

It carried different payloads into low earth orbit. It provided crew rotation for the International Space Station (ISS). It also performed servicing missions. The orbiter could recover satellites and other payloads from orbit and return them to Earth. Each Shuttle was designed for a projected lifespan of 100 launches or ten years of operational life, although this was later extended. The crucial factor in the size and shape of the Shuttle Orbiter was the requirement that it be able to accommodate the largest planned commercial and military satellites. The Shuttle's cross-range recovery capability also met all the requirements for classified USAF missions.

However, the original design of the Shuttle's sophisticated communications system did not include a strategic security capability required to support all DoD missions. This capability would provide a classified level of encryption for all voice, data, and telemetry communications.

The development of the complex ground-based and space-borne equipment required to accomplish the retrofit of the Space Shuttle with this capability was started in the late 1970's and code-named Project Elwell.

The Elwell development and initial production contract was competitively awarded to the Government Electronics Division of Motorola, Inc. The technical challenge involved the design & development of the ground-based and space-borne encryption equipment as well as the monumental task of coordinating the effort with the associated tri-services (Army, Navy and Air Force) projects. The Elwell project team would also have to design the equipment such that it could be physically and electronically retrofitted into a "fixed-footprint" or form factor which was dictated by the original design of the Space Shuttle vehicle.

A couple of years prior to the planned launch of STS-51-C, the difficult development effort was successfully completed and tested. By 1982, the focus had shifted to the critical delivery of the production grade equipment required to retrofit the Space Shuttle fleet and ensure that the first planned DoD mission could be accomplished on schedule.

The Elwell production contract was also awarded to Motorola's Government Electronics Division. Motorola would organize the project into a matrix-managed program team to accomplish the contract's objectives. That is, a team comprised of hundreds of engineering, manufacturing, materials procurement, quality management and production professionals reporting to a single Elwell Production Program Manager, but only on a dotted-line basis. The production team members would get their direction from the Program Manager for the execution of the Elwell Production contract but still report to their respective functional departments for performance and salary reviews.

This Elwell production team would eventually manufacture and deliver many highly reliable ground-based and space-borne units on multiple contracts exceeding $100 million over several years. This would include, of course, the successful delivery of the equipment required to enable the January 24, 1985 launch of Space Shuttle Discovery and the STS-51-C mission.

The Elwell Production Program team also succeeded in establishing itself as a high-performance team within Motorola. The team exceeded all internal quality goals despite difficult material procurement challenges. The Elwell Production team was one of the first production teams to be awarded over a million dollars in special performance bonuses based on exceeding pre-determined quality and cost reduction targets.

I feel privileged to have had the opportunity to serve as the Elwell Production Program Manager and to lead the Elwell Production team during this momentous period. As a relatively new Program Manager, this was my first major experience in leading a multifaceted mix of professional talent in a true matrix management environment. At its peak, my expanded Elwell Production team numbered over 300 team members.

We were able to maintain an intense focus on executing a complex project under intense schedule pressure and design constraints. I quickly learned that leading this type of team, without the authority of a "solid line" reporting relationship, required me to prepare myself for every turn along the way. After some initial "ego bruising" and unexpected disappointments, I realized that in order to be successful in this particular leadership role, I would have to build the team's trust in my ability to articulate the "big picture" as well as the details surrounding the technical and production challenges. I would also have to confidently lead with enduring intention.

With a peer leadership team spanning much of NASA, DoD (including the Army, Air Force, Navy) and the National Security Agency, keeping a flawless focus on the project's purpose was a must. Just as important was the need for me to envision, from the start, how the project would end and keep a laser focus on the path to success.

I made it a point during every morning "stand-up" meeting with the Elwell Production team to clearly update everyone on our purpose, our goals, our status, and our daily & monthly objectives.

At 30 years of age, I found myself regularly engaging with talented engineers and skilled production assembly team members as well as three-star military Generals. I was fully cognizant of and respected the fact that I was viewed, at all levels, as the final decision-maker regarding critical performance requirements and delivery commitments. I realized that I was not just the Production Program Manager. I was the designated leader of a passionate, cross-functional team that was depending on me and my leadership to ensure the project's success.

When the Space Shuttle Discovery touched down at 4:23 p.m. EST on January 27, 1985, it also brought home 385 special Elwell badges that traveled the complete 1.3 million miles of the mission. A few months after the successful STS-51-C mission, I was proud to be a part of a recognition ceremony where each of the Elwell Production team members were given one of these special badges.

To this day, I place extraordinary value on the badge I received that day and on the lessons in leadership I learned during that stage of my management career.

LEADERSHIP FRONT AND CENTER

THIS IS WHAT MAKES MY DAYS MOST MEMORABLE. WHAT ABOUT YOURS?

"Dr. Fay Cobb Payton believes that having leadership teams that represent a broad "intersection" of the world's population is critical to navigating the increasing diversity of the 21st-century workforce."
--- Janette Braverman, Owner of Leaders Leaving Legacies, LLC

Published on May 12, 2020

Almost to the day, seven years ago this month, I had the opportunity to spend some time in Atlanta with the Information Technology Senior Management Forum. The Information Technology Senior Management Forum (ITSMF) was established in 1996. As I understand it, the national organization began with a conversation between a few prominent technology executives after realizing that black professionals were holding only three to four percent of Information Technology Management roles in the U.S.

The ITSMF mission soon became one that *"increases the representation of black professionals at senior levels in technology, [all] to impact organizational innovation and growth."* After learning more about the organization, I found the most intriguing aspect of their mission is their focus on achieving its mission by *"developing and nurturing dynamic leaders [currently within companies] through [the] enrichment of the mind, body and soul."*

I accepted an invitation from the ITSMF to come to Atlanta and give the keynote address during one of their annual Management Academy Graduation Ceremonies. I must admit that it was quite a "memorable" moment. I had just loss my father in February of 2013 and I needed to take a break, get away from my surroundings in Phoenix and enjoy the presence of some energetic high achievers.

The speech I gave that night to the graduating class and their guests was also quite "memorable". It was a speech written especially for the occasion. I titled the seventeen-minute speech *Swapportunity*. I wanted to empathize the need to recognize the importance of the "present moment" and to realize when you have the opportunity to "swap" who you are today with who you wish to become in the future.

The genesis of my message was a lesson I had learned after spending over 15 years as a technology executive with Motorola and the Wells Fargo Bank. I challenged the Class of 2013 to recognize the importance of the *present moment* and to not *hesitate* to take advantage of the opportunity to "swap" the roles they presently hold – for the senior management roles (i.e. CEO, CIO, Director) they wish to hold in the future.

Both the opportunity to spend some time with the ITSMF and share one of my best messages with the Management Academy Class of 2013 are high on my list of "memorable" moments.

However, nothing like the type of moment I experienced yesterday afternoon.

Yesterday afternoon, I experienced what I call a *"legacy moment."*

That is, those moments that instantly registers as "most memorable – at later stages in life.

You see, earlier today, I received a LinkedIn message from someone that I met while working out in the hotel exercise room back in May 2013 --- the morning following my Friday night presentation to the ITSMF Management Academy Class. In a delightful conversation, she shared some of the work she had done over the years in her doctorate level studies of what is called "intersectionality."

If you are like me, I had no idea --- at the time --- what she was talking about.

The initial conversation turned into future discussions where Dr. Fay shared a ton of her terrific and pioneering work in this area of study. The publishing arm of my company reviewed her work and offered her a publishing contract. This would be her first book and the first time such an extensive compilation of her outstanding work would be shared with the entire world. In August 2014, Dr. Fay Cobb Payton (no direct family relationship to my family) and RICHER Press published her book titled, *Leveraging Intersectionality: Seeing and Not Seeing.*

Intersectionality is a topic worthy of learning more about and understanding its impact within organizations and throughout society.

In her unexpected message to me this afternoon, Dr. Fay excitedly shared with me a Forbes.com article recently published titled, *How Women of Color Can Advocate for Themselves in the Workplace.* In the article, Dr. Fay is prominently quoted, and her book is highly referenced.

Now, why was the moment I experienced yesterday afternoon a "legacy moment" for me?

Well, when my partners and I established Richer Life, LLC back in 2010, we all agreed that our sole mission would be to *"shape thoughts and change lives for the better"*. After investing in dozens of promising authors over the past decade, every time I hear about how our work may be realizing our mission...it makes my day most memorable and reminds me of some of my legacy.

When you reflect on the work YOU have done over the past decade...what kind of message can you receive – today – that would make your day "most memorable"?

Thanks Fay.

How to Lead with Intention and Not Authority

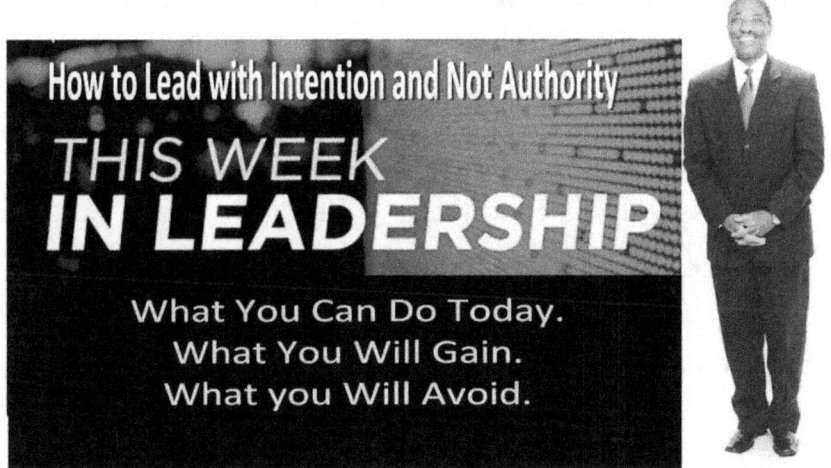

Published on May 8, 2020

I must admit that when I was promoted to my first leadership position I was not aware that there were so many documented leadership styles.

From Autocratic to Democratic to Laissez-faire and from Mahatma Gandhi to Winston Churchill to Martin Luther King, there are as many leadership styles as there are leaders. Most experts in the field of leadership would agree that to become a more effective leader, it is important to develop your own, personal leadership style.

Common to all styles of leadership is the availability and the use of authority. Of course, some level of authority is essential to achieve leadership success within any organizational context. This is especially the case when it comes to managing situations across and up the organizational structure.

However, my personal experience overwhelmingly suggests that to lead more effectively those in the organization below you to the best possible outcome, gaining their respect and commitment through clarity of direction and mutual expectations is essential.

Leading with intention means that your ultimate goal as a leader is to add value to your organization, gain the commitment of others and develop & deploy all the talents of your team members --- all while sustaining loyalty.

How can you lead with intention?

Here is what you can do today, what you will gain and what you will avoid.

LEADING WITH INTENTION, NOT AUTHORITY

WHAT TO DO TODAY	WHAT YOU WILL GAIN	WHAT YOU WILL AVOID
Express clearly your wants, needs and desires.	Being perceived as a visionary who knows what is needed to achieve the team's goals.	Organizational confusion regarding what is needed and what you desire.
Go out of your way to show respect for other's points of view.	The trust and mutual respect of your team.	The perception that only your point of view matters.
Listen with intent to understand what is really being said.	Valuable insight into what your team is really thinking.	Being "blind-sided" by what your team thinks of you.
Take the time to appraise your team's talents and developmental needs.	The vision you need to effectively deploy and develop your team.	Not having the talent and skills required to accomplish your goals.
Appraise any skills deficiencies you may have which might impact your success on this particular challenge.	The insight needed to devise a timely plan to "plug-the-holes" and increase the probability of success.	Not being prepared for the task at hand. Having only "four-cylinders" when "six cylinders" are needed.

LEADERSHIP FRONT AND CENTER

A Key Post COVID-19 Leadership Lesson: Things Change - But Not Humanity

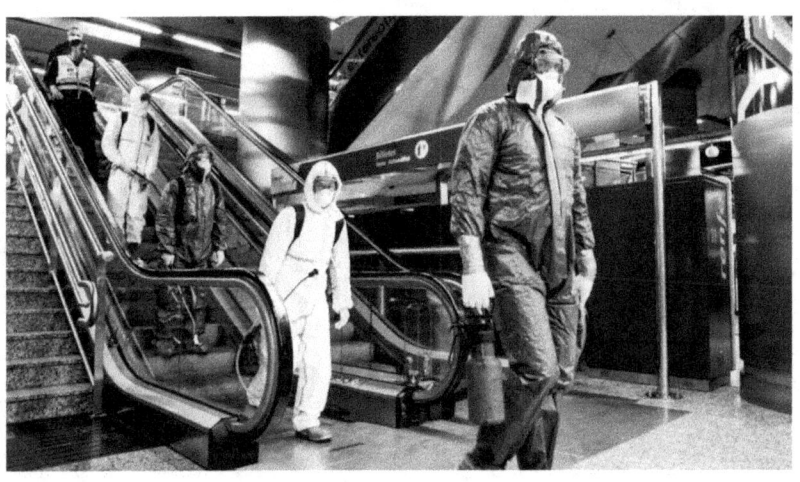

Published on May 4, 2020

Right now, it feels impossible to predict what the world will look like next week, let alone next year. Yet behavioral science and the broad sweep of history suggest that COVID-19 will transform all our daily lives in the long run – including how we "lead" our teams and our organizations.

Some of the changes in "what we do" are already in progress and started as soon as case counts, and deaths began to escalate.

I recently read a University of Southern California study which stated that COVID-19 (the coronavirus we are currently dealing with) had already created significant shifts in people's "general" behavior. The study found that 85 percent of people reported washing their hands or using sanitizer more often than before, and 61 percent reported following social distancing guidelines.

During some down time this past weekend – and like most of you, I have had more down time in the last month that I have had in 20 years – I began to think about how the changes in people caused by this COVID-19 pandemic could affect my ability to lead my project teams and my organization, in general.

As you know, I have been studying and writing about "organizational leadership" and "project leadership" for over 10 years now...since the day I handed in my Blackberry to the Wells Fargo Bank and said goodbye to my 34 year corporate career.

Therefore, to feed my curiosity and understand how a pandemic could impact how leaders lead, I immediately began to dig into this interesting new topic by asking the question:

What changes in my "leadership fundamentals" and/or "leadership style" must occur for me to continue to be an effective leader in the Post COVID-19 era?

I started this thought process by first, standing back and reminding myself of the basic and fundamental understanding of both *leadership* and *humanity*.

Why humanity you ask?

Well, as leaders, we all should never forget that *leadership* is about leading other human being.

Leadership, simply put, is the act of guiding, encouraging and motivating others to achieve a common vision or goal.

The word **humanity**, of course, encompasses the entire human race, which includes everyone on Earth. However, to most Anthropologists (the scientists who studies humans, human behavior and societies in the past and present), the word "humanity" refers to the *qualities* that make us human, such as the ability to love and have compassion, be creative, and not be a robot or alien.

Following many hours of research and thought, it finally hit me. At that moment, I realized that I had just learned what will be a key leadership lesson as it relates to being an effective leader in the post COVID-19 era.

Frankly, I am almost embarrassed to have spent so much time to research this question and arrive to this enlightened *understanding*. However, I do not believe that I will be the only person to over think this question over the next few months.

Here is the lesson I learned.

If you are currently an effective team or organizational leader --- no changes are required.

Why, you ask?

Well, because *effective* leadership is all about taking the time to understand and get to know each of your team members as the *unique humans* that they are.

Effective leaders are trained and prepared to provide support, trust, motivation, clarity, encouragement, and empathy to all team members.

History has proven that for centuries now...from one corner of the earth to the other – *"things Change, but not humanity"*.

"Then, I woke up again...and realized that many Americans were most likely focusing on "self, family, health and near-term economic survival" at the time."

LEADERSHIP FRONT AND CENTER

BEING PRESENT WHEN DECISIONS ARE BEING MADE DURING "UNCERTAIN" TIMES

Published on April 25, 2020

It only takes a quick review of American history to see how Congressional and Presidential decisions made during times of "national uncertainty" have minimized opportunities for generations of Americans and have helped to shape the America as we know it today.

On Friday morning "I suddenly woke up" in a sweat from an unthinkable dream.

In the dream, a "novel" coronavirus was attacking almost every corner of the earth and for some reason the United States was leading the world in infections (over 900,000 cases) and deaths (over 52,000), as of today.

Then, I got out of bed and realized that I was not dreaming.

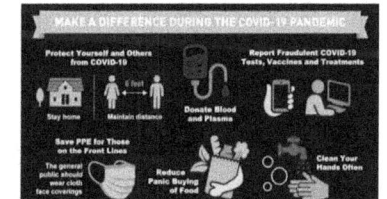

Like most of you, to help our country get through the COVID-19 pandemic with minimum social and

economic impact, my wife and I have a list of "things-to-do"
Our list includes:
- Wearing face masks, washing our hands frequently and using disinfectants.
- Respecting our distance when around others.
- Staying home as much as possible; and
- Obeying orders and suggestions from local and national leaders.

We both see being "absent – that is a deliberate or accidental failure to do what we should do – as a dereliction of our duty as Americans.

However, as I was doing some research this weekend I realized that our list was missing an important item:

The need for us to pay attention to the decisions that our Congressional and Executive branches of government are making during this "time of uncertainty" – while the vast majority of the population is focused on "self, family, health and near-term economic survival."

Why is this so important you ask?

This is important because "transformative" chapters of our American history include some major decisions that were made by our Congressional and Executive branches of government during times of "uncertainty". At the time, these critical decisions may have appeared to be "rational and/or necessary" to maintain our "Federation".

However, in decades of hindsight, these decisions now are viewed by most historians as having "detrimental" impact to our nation as a whole.

As I researched this list of critical decisions, I kept asking myself:
- *What was most Americans doing when such decisions were being made? and*

- *Why couldn't they see the long-term impact and the lack of humanity rolled into many of the decisions?*

Then, I "woke up" again – and realized that many Americans were most likely focusing on "self, family, health and near-term economic survival" at the time.

The list includes decisions that have affected many aspects of our lives as Americans – from disparities in education and healthcare to the "lock" that the top 1% has on the American economy and the political discourse.

Here are two of the decisions that I believe have had the most lasting impact on shaping and maintaining the America as we know it today.

1. **DECISION: The decision made by the U.S. Congress around the "uncertainly" of the intensely disputed 1876 presidential election, which resulted in the Compromise of 1877.**

The Compromise of 1877 was one of a series of political compromises reached during the 19th century to hold the United States together peacefully. What made the Compromise of 1877 unique was that it took place after the Civil War and was thus an attempt to prevent a second outbreak of violence.

The Affect:

Over the next three decades following the Compromise, the civil rights that blacks had been promised during Reconstruction crumbled under white rule in the south. For about 100 years, from the Post-civil War era until 1968, Jim Crow Laws were in place in the U.S. – Laws meant to marginalize African Americans by denying them the right to vote, hold jobs, get an education or other opportunities.

Today, more than one-in-five voting members (22%) of the U.S. House of Representatives and Senate are racial or ethnic minorities. The number makes the 116th Congress the most racially and ethnically diverse in history.

Just Think:

What might this percentage be today if Reconstruction (the Thirteenth, Fourteenth and Fifteenth Amendments to the U.S. Constitution) was defended then as strongly and the Second Amendment is defended today?

Growing racial and ethnic diversity in Congress

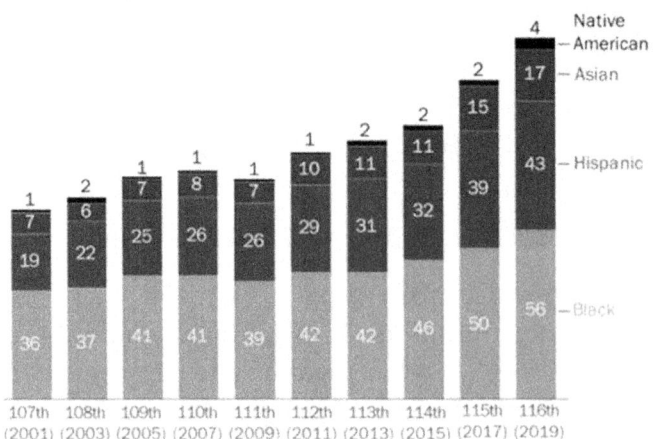

LEADERSHIP FRONT AND CENTER

2. **DECISION:** The September 30, 1918 decision by President Woodrow Wilson to formally and publicly support granting voting rights to women following the increasing "uncertainly" and unrest (women's suffrage movement) surrounding the right of women to vote.

The Affect:

Fifty-two years after the introduction of the first amendment legalizing voting for women, the United States Congress "finally" passed the 19th Amendment, giving that right to all  women in the U.S. The amendment was ratified on August 18, 1920. Today, only 23% of the United States House of Representatives and the Senate are women...while women make up 51% of the U.S. population.

Just Think:

What might this percentage be today if the "women right to vote" was established back in the 1800s?

Without a doubt, we all should focus on "self, family, health and near-term economic survival" during this COVID-19 pandemic.

However, as participants in **THIS** Chapter of American history, we should also commit to being **"PRESENT"** and **NOT ABSENT** when national decisions are being made during today's "uncertain" times.

LEADERSHIP FRONT AND CENTER

Organizational Leadership in a Post COVID-19 World - A Need for Everyone to Step Up Their Game

Published on April 15, 2020

According to the experts, beginning in December 2019, in the region of Wuhan, China, a new ("novel") coronavirus began appearing in human beings. It has been named COVID-19, a shortened form of "coronavirus disease of 2019." This new virus spreads incredibly quickly between people, due to its newness – no one on earth has an immunity to COVID-19, because no one had COVID-19 until 2019.

To put the global impact that these viruses can have in perspective, let us recall the 1918 influenza pandemic. It was the most severe pandemic in recent history. It was caused by an H1N1 virus with genes of avian origin. Although there is not universal consensus regarding where the virus originated, it spread worldwide during 1918-1919. In the United States, it was first identified in military personnel in spring 1918. It is estimated that about 500 million people or one-third of the world's population became infected with this virus. The number of deaths was estimated to be at least 50 million worldwide with about 675,000 occurring in the United States.

Back then, with "no vaccine" to protect against this influenza infection and no antibiotics to treat secondary bacterial infections that can be associated with influenza infections, control efforts worldwide were limited to non-pharmaceutical interventions such as isolation, quarantine, good personal hygiene, use of disinfectants, and limitations of public gatherings, which were applied unevenly.

Does this sound familiar with what we are hearing today (i.e. stay home, wash your hand frequently, practice social distancing)?

This morning I read in several different sources about how effective the "social distancing" practice has been in reducing the current COVID-19 infection rate and saving American lives. Of course, it has come with the need to shut down a large portion of the U.S. economy and affecting everyone's daily life.

However, some more sobering reports indicate that without more insight into the nature of COVID-19 and an effective vaccine, it may take up to 18 months or longer before things get back to what we once considered "normal" in the United States.

In an attempt to keep certain aspects of our lives functioning, many "essential" companies and government agencies have had to significantly expand the use of "virtual" and "limited personal contact" options as a means of providing the required level of trust, management, direction, communication, accountability, encouragement and empathy to lead organizations and individuals during such uncertain times.

Chances are that this virtual and limited personal contact approach to the workplace, work culture and organizational leadership (within large companies and organizations as well as functional and project teams) will become a "new normal" for quite some time into the future.

There has been talk about the U.S. economy springing back to normal is short order. Yet, to even get close to emulating the level of productivity, performance, efficiency, and overall success of the last few years, many believe that both team members and their leaders must "step up their game." By this, I mean that there will be a need for *performers* to perform at their very best and their *leader*s to become *outstanding leaders*.

Based on what is generally known about leading small and large teams in a mostly virtual environment, I believe that there are five key leadership attributes, which tend to play a larger role than normal in helping to obtain better results when being "face-to-face" is not possible and during uncertain times.

They are:

1. Leads by Example
2. Strong Communicator
3. Respectfully Open-Minded
4. Calm and in Control
5. Truly Nurturing

Many of you may believe you are familiar with each of these attributes and feel that you are either capable of applying &

benefiting from them – or – know exactly how to "step up your game" in these areas when necessary.

However, I would like to challenge you to review each of the attributes at the end of this article for a brief *"What I should be doing and Why"* overview or reminder.

You might just learn a little about what is required to be an *outstanding leader* and a lot about yourself.

You may also find the insights "transformational" as you join all of us in "stepping up our leadership game" over the next few months.

Be safe and be honestly mindful of what is in front of you.

LEADS BY EXAMPLE
Transformation Framework

1. I am sensitive to team member's feelings and am always kind to them.	Everyone has a rough day, or a day when everything seems to go wrong. Outstanding Leaders are sensitive during these times and supportive of their team.
2. I take time to make team members feel special.	They all want to feel special. Outstanding Leaders take the time to sincerely praise their teams for things that they do.
3. I listen to each Team Member's emotions as well as words.	Remember that 60 to 90 percent of our communication is nonverbal. Outstanding Leaders read their Team Members' body language as well as their emotions.
4. I perceive each Team Member's needs and wants as being valid.	Instead of jumping to the conclusion that a Team Member can survive quite well without the things that *they say are needed*, Outstanding Leaders take the position that the request is valid, and then do everything in their power to respond.
5. I choose my battles wisely.	Outstanding Leaders do not waste their time and energy engaging in fights that have no consequence or that will leave them drained.
6. I respect all Team Member differences.	Each one of us is unique. Outstanding Leaders consider their *Team Members'* differences when they make decisions that affect them.
7. I avoid being defensive and placing Team Members on the defensive.	Outstanding Leaders do not take honest feedback personally--they learn from it and use it to improve. When they provide feedback to their Team Members, they make sure that it is candid, fair, and honest, and helps the Team Member find ways to use it to improve.
8. I give Team Members the benefit of the doubt.	No one goes to work each day wanting to do a terrible job. Outstanding Leaders assume that each one of their Team Members is a good and honest person who wants to do the best job possible.

9. I resolve interpersonal problems as quickly as possible.	Outstanding Leaders should not let disagreements or hurt feelings fester. They get these issues out into the open and work to resolve them quickly.
10. I treat Team Members the way I would like to be treated.	Outstanding Leaders know how they would like to be treated by others and they do the same for their Team Members.

"The reality is that the only way change comes is when you lead by example."

— Anne Wojcicki

STRONG COMMUNICATOR
Transformation Framework

1. When I communicate with others, I am aware of my inner monologue.	All good communication starts from a place of self-awareness. When Outstanding Leaders communicate with others, they are always aware of their inner monologue. They always assume the other person can read their mind and can sense if they are being discriminatory or appearing unconfident.
2. When I communicate with others, I make sure that I know my audience.	The best communication arises out of understanding your audience. Outstanding Leaders always know their audience's motivations, preferred communication styles, learning styles. This allows them to adapt their messages and increase the odds of effective communication.
3. When I communicate with others, I am direct, specific and clear.	Clear-cut communication increases the likelihood that people will comprehend and take action on whatever you are asking from them. Outstanding Leaders know that it is better to "over-explain" something than to leave room for misunderstanding.
4. When I communicate with others, I pay attention to my nonverbal communication.	Plenty of research suggests nonverbal communication is just as important as what a person says—maybe even more. Outstanding Leaders know that facial expressions, hand gestures, posture and eye contact all play a major role in affirming or undermining their messages.
5. When I communicate with others, I listen more than I speak.	One of the best ways to encourage open and honest communication within a group is to model active listening. Outstanding Leaders know that when someone is speaking to them, they should really listen to what is being said. They also ask follow-up questions to demonstrate that they are paying attention and to make sure there are no miscommunications. They also keep an open mind and focus on thoughtfully responding to what has been said. This practice builds rapport and understanding.

STRONG COMMUNICATOR
Transformation Framework

6. When I communicate with others, I am always positive and respectful.	Outstanding Leaders always prioritize transparent, fair and respectful communication within a group. They know that this is one of the best strategies for cultivating loyalty and boosting the team's performance. They do not hold their status over other people or use coercion or fear as motivators. Instead, they focus on bringing honest, positive and egoless attitudes to every situation that arises. Serving as a cheerleader instead of an autocrat helps maintain morale and can even facilitate creativity and effective problem solving.

"The art of communication is the language of leadership."

— James Humes

OPEN-MINDED
Transformation Framework

1. I am open to accepting as well as giving.	Outstanding Leaders have the ability to think of things from various angles and viewpoints. This allows them to accept more and take advantage of different ways to accomplish needed outcomes.
2. I am willing to embrace change.	All Outstanding Leaders are willing and able to embrace change with open arms because they see various possibilities and outcomes, rather than judging it from only one angle of "experience".
3. I have a high level of curiosity.	All Outstanding Leaders have a natural ability to want to know more about something. They tend not to judge an idea that may be presented to them with only what they know. They prefer to inquire, learn and discover new insights.
4. I am willing to try new things.	Outstanding Leaders value new ideas and trying new things. They do not mind trying out a new place for dinner, or making new friends, or embracing a new project.
5. I do not judge people or ideas without first listening attentively.	Outstanding Leaders are willing to listen to someone without judging them or jumping to conclusions before they have finished.
6. I am always open to other's opinions.	It is okay to be opinionated. However, Outstanding Leaders have a good understanding of the fact that they do not have to agree with everyone or vice versa.
7. I always respect differences in people and personalities.	All Outstanding Leaders are open to people's values, beliefs, and differences. They believe that differences are what make everyone unique— which is a valuable quality.
8. I primarily live in the present and not the past.	Outstanding Leaders do not dwell on the past. They trust that everything happens for a reason. Furthermore, they try not to fret over the future because they see so many possible outcomes. Focusing on the present and appreciating those moments is seen as far more sensible to them.

OPEN-MINDED
Transformation Framework

9. I routinely turn problems into opportunities.	Outstanding Leaders acknowledge the fact that every problem has a solution or at least a different perspective that is better than the first. This enables them to see clearly when faced with difficult situations and tackle problems without panicking. For them, problems are opportunities to learn what to fix.

"Without an open-minded mind, you can never be a great success."

— *Martha Stewart*

CALM
Transformation Framework

1. When facing challenging situations, I stop or pause first before responding.	Outstanding Leaders will give themselves a little extra time before saying or doing something. It is very tempting in stressful situations to react quickly and say or do the first thing that comes to mind, however they know that it is more beneficial to pause first, then respond.
2. In highly stressful situations, I automatically take a break.	In highly stressful situations, Outstanding Leaders know that taking a break and allowing others involved to do the same, will dissipate any built up tension. It is quite amazing how much clearer they can think when they step away from something that has been bothering them.
3. I often calm down by taking time to reflect.	Outstanding Leaders know that self-reflection is a powerful skill for anyone to have. During reflection, it gives them the opportunity to check their attitude and determine whether what they are doing is what is required at that time. They, quite often, reflect to help them see things from different perspectives, which can help them reach solutions quicker.
4. I normally refocus on the direction of all of my projects as progress is made.	Outstanding Leaders know that the lack of clarity results in confusion, which can often cloud their judgement and their ability to make good decisions. Just asking, "What am I trying to accomplish right now?" helps them get back to what is most important at the time.
5. I consider myself resolute and I hold high convictions in face of adversity.	When challenged with a difficult issue requiring a prompt solution, Outstanding Leaders know that being caught up in one way of doing things can continue to create more pressure for them and those involved. When they start asking new questions, they will be forced to come up with new answers. In order to get new results, they have to take new actions and it starts with asking new questions.

LEADERSHIP FRONT AND CENTER

CALM
Transformation Framework

6. I make it a point to speak to a mentor or trusted advisor when I face new and unfamiliar challenges.	Almost all the challenges we will ever face in life, someone has already faced. Outstanding Leaders know that instead of trying to work out everything on their own or even try to force something to happen, it can be beneficial to speak to a mentor or trusted advisor. They will be able to share new perspectives that will often help make the situation a lot easier to address.
7. When I find myself under stress, I try to change my self-talk.	Outstanding Leaders know that most stress is self-created and it often starts with their self-talk. If we consistently have negative self-talk, we will tend to experience negative emotions. Instead of being our own worst critic, it is more beneficial to change our self-talk to one that is encouraging, positive and focused on outcomes.

"Calm mind brings inner strength and self-confidence, so that's very important for good health."

— Dalai Lama

NURTURING
Transformation Framework

1. I am supportive of team members seeking more professional training and development.	Outstanding Leaders know that each team member brings some level of experience and knowledge to the project. They also know that effective training is how to best integrate a team member's existing knowledge into the project's plan and strategy.
2. I frequently look for opportunities to provide team members increased responsibility.	Outstanding Leaders know that providing team members with opportunities to take on additional responsibility will show them how much they trust them.
3. I always "connect the dots" regarding how each team member brings value to the project.	Outstanding Leaders make it a point to help "connect the dots" regarding each team member's contribution to the project. Connecting the dots means explaining why each team member and task is extremely important to the mission of the project.
4. I always recognize achievements and show my appreciation for good performance.	Outstanding Leaders are committed and dedicated to the project team. Thanking their team and giving honest recognition for the team's work achievements can help the team to feel appreciated and enhance their job satisfaction.
5. I find ways to create a learning project culture.	Professional development and growth happens where people are encouraged to be curious and learn. Outstanding Leaders provide feedback regularly and allow team members the space to explore new ideas or solutions. Not only does a learning-oriented culture help to cultivate leadership, it also breeds innovation and high-performance.
6. I always establish and clearly communicate project and team goals.	How can you prepare your team members for leadership if you don't know what their goals are? In addition to giving them a better understanding of how each individual fits into the Team as a whole, Outstanding Leaders also take time to understand personal goals.

LEADERSHIP FRONT AND CENTER

NURTURING
Transformation Framework

7. I promote professional growth among my team members by encouraging and providing stretch goals.	Professional growth is uncomfortable and challenging. Outstanding Leaders know that creativity and innovation are born out of the need to stretch beyond a team member's comfort zone to accomplish a goal and that achieving stretch-goals successfully can be a great confidence booster.
8. I consider myself a role model to my team members.	Intentionally or not, the Leaders within an organization demonstrate the characteristics they cultivate in their teams. Outstanding Leaders know that it is important for them to intentionally model the kinds of behavior they expect from all team members.
9. I make sure that I do not neglect poor performance.	Poor performance is usually a sign of disengagement and that something is not working. Outstanding Leaders know that it is important to provide the team members with the opportunity to improve, along with actions to be taken. This does not have to be a punitive experience. If Outstanding Leaders see everyone with the potential of improving their performance, they help everyone to do their best work.

"Management is about arranging and telling. Leadership is about nurturing and enhancing."

— Tom Peters

LEADERSHIP FRONT AND CENTER

WHY LEADERSHIP DURING A CRISIS LIKE THE CORONAVIRUS DEMANDS EMPATHY

Published on March 17, 2020

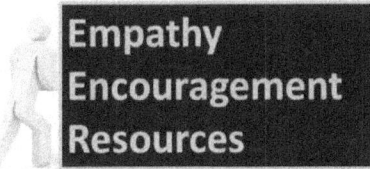

When many good managers and organizational leaders talk about leadership and being a leader, you will often hear words such as strong, strategic, passionate, confident, focused, mindful, committed and energetic.

These words are among a list of words most often used to describe leaders and leadership traits. They are also among the words that you most likely would expect to hear. However, have you ever heard the word empathetic when you hear managers and leaders talk about leadership?

Over the years, I have learned through my experiences and the experiences of many others that, over time, empathy becomes one of the most important traits you must have as a leader. Empathetic leaders can better understand their associates and team members' skill sets, their aspirations, their concerns, and their needs – particularly in times of crisis.

During a crisis like the concerns of the current Coronavirus, we must think of empathy as the ability to experience and relate to the thoughts, emotions, and fears of others. Empathy is more than sympathy — which simple allows you to understand and support others with compassion or sensitivity.

For many reasons, many good managers and organizational leaders lack an adequate level of empathy and are not able to be empathetic when the situation demands it. Thus, they fail to reap the significant dividends that can be reaped from being a skilled, competent and empathic leader.

Here are the most common shortcomings I have found that can prevent the development of this critical leadership trait:

- The failure to make the critical distinction between being sympathetic and being empathetic.
- The failure to gain the capacity to control, express and be mindful of their own emotions. This impacts their ability to empathetically handle interpersonal relationships; and
- The failure to be professionally thoughtful and pay attention to the "why" behind an associate or team member's perspective, in terms of differences in gender, race, ethnicity, economic status and/or culture.

Here are a few actions you can take:

1. Talk About Empathy

Let associates and team members know that empathy matters. Explain how giving time and attention to others in the organization fosters empathy, which in turn can enhance everyone's performance and improve organizational effectiveness.

2. Rethink How You Listen

To understand others and sense what they are feeling, you must be an active listener. Active listeners let others know that they are being heard, by non-verbally expressing an understanding of concerns and problems. When their leader is a good listener, team members feel respected and professional trust can develop and grow.

3. Seek and Learn from the Perspectives of Others

Empathetic leaders learn and gain valuable insights by actively seeking and assessing the perspectives of others. The assessment should include taking into consideration the individual's personal experiences, gender, racial, ethnic and/or cultural differences.

As we execute our leadership responsibilities during the current Coronavirus crisis, we must remember that our primary responsibility over the next few weeks, or months, is to provide the empathy, encouragement and resources that only we, as our organization's leaders, can provide.

"Just as most people...successful Professionals start out having no intention of making a change...in their lives, in their jobs or in their careers. Then, something happens..."

LEADERSHIP FRONT AND CENTER

MANAGING CHANGE REQUIRES A NEW PLAYBOOK FOR SUCCESS

Published on March 7, 2020

What is the one thing I have in common with Nashville, Seattle, Dayton, Gaithersburg, Charlotte, Phoenix and Savannah?

Well...over the past forty-years and through various stages of my life and career, I have once called each of these places HOME.

Yes. My wife and I will soon call the historic, vibrate and growing city of Savannah, Georgia home. However, after almost four decades together, we now have a proven playbook for managing the most importance aspects of making a successful change: "Changing Behavior" and "Changing Mindset". I am sure that you are all familiar with or have heard of the six stages of "behavioral" change.

1) Pre-Contemplation
2) Contemplation
3) Preparation
4) Action
5) Maintenance
6) Relapse

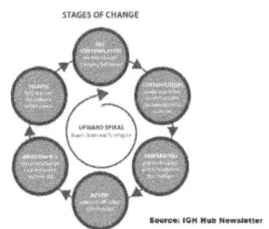

Most successful professionals start out with no intention of making a change – in their lives, in their jobs or in their careers.

Then, something happens...dissatisfaction, slow career growth, job misalignment, lack of organizational mobility, internal conflict or an unexpected change in their work environment – and not making a change is not an option. The upward spiral of behavioral adjustments and finally acceptance leads to a platform for success during the next stage of their personal and professional lives. Quickly learning from "relapses" is key to establishing a sustainable change in behavior.

However, we have learned that a sustainable change in "behavior" without a corresponding change in "mindset" can be problematic. The change in "mindset" (i.e. your established set of attitudes) is a critical part of completing any change. A mindset that does not fully embrace and embody the characteristics of the new environment typically results in short-lived and substandard performance and success.

We have also found that one of the most effective methods to gain this critical change in mindset – one that will fully release your personal and professional strengths – is one, which takes specific and overt "actions" on your part.

We have summarized these actions within an acronym that has held a prominent position in our playbook for success for years.

The acronym is H.O.M.E.

Have confidence in your ability and experience. (You have paid the price, reap the rewards.)

Own the responsibility to take the initiative to let people know who you are. (Tell your own story.)

Move quickly and methodically into available roles of leadership and responsibility. (People believe what they SEE and not what you SAY.)

Envision the most successful and broadest possible outcomes. (Remember, if you can think it, you can do it.)

If you are contemplating a change (of any type) which moves you in the direction you currently desire --- go for it.

Just remember -- first change your behavior to adjust to your new environment and then, change your mindset – by going H.O.M.E.

Savannah here we come. Not just to visit this time.

We are again, bringing H.O.M.E to a new home.

"Gaining the leadership skills required to be an effective leader within your organization does not occur overnight."

LEADERSHIP FRONT AND CENTER

The Natural Progression to Mastering Leadership Skills

Published on March 4, 2020

No one is born a highly skilled organizational leader. Gaining the leadership skills required to be an effective leader within your organization does not occur overnight. It requires taking the time to understand what is required to be successful.

The best way to do this is to closely observe others in the organization that are or have been successful in leadership roles.

Then, it requires you to embrace the fundamental changes in your broad approach to leading with an acceptance of one key reality:

Becoming a respected and trustworthy leader in today's diverse, complex and global organizations represent challenges that did not exist in the past.

Even for seasoned managers, making the necessary adjustments and learning new organizational leadership skills typically involves a natural progression. When the new skill involves performing a known task in a new and better manner, the following learning progression is necessary and typical.

Unconsciously Incompetent

In a nutshell, everyone starts out not knowing what they don't know.

Therefore, you do not recognize that you do not know what you are doing because you do not know what you are supposed to be doing to get the leadership results needed. Regardless of your current leadership skills --- you can be better and gain even better results - for you and your organization.

Consciously Incompetent

This state is typically the result of an educational experience.

Through continuous learning, you come to realize that there are leadership skills and knowledge that you need to be more effective in your current organizational culture that you do not possess at the necessary levels. This realization is key to becoming motivated to gain the required skills.

Consciously Competent

This state is a natural result of focused learning.

You recognize there are required leadership skills you need, and you have learned what those skills are and when they are best applied.

You are capable of putting these skills into action. However, doing so requires conscious thought on your part. You know what to do, when to do it and how to do it but to get it right you must mentally focus on the effort. Your new leadership skills are not yet mastered to the point of being a competitive advantage.

Unconsciously Competent

Education, new leadership skills, experience, time and practice yields significantly enhanced results and rewards --- both organizationally and personally.

When your new leadership skills can be applied via focused action, taken correctly and immediately without any thought or consideration at all on your part, then you have become an unconsciously competent and a skilled organizational leader.

Regardless of the business challenge or project target at hand, you shine as a leader – right now – without any conscious thought at all.

Remember, becoming a respected and trustworthy leader in today's diverse, complex, and global organizations represent challenges that did not exist in the past.

Therefore, get through your progression and shine.

"I opened the case and found that the DVD contained a copy of the actual interview I gave almost ten years ago while attending a church in North Scottsdale. The church has since changed its name to Impact Church."

LEADERSHIP FRONT AND CENTER

HIGH-PERFORMERS - YOU CAN'T PARK THERE

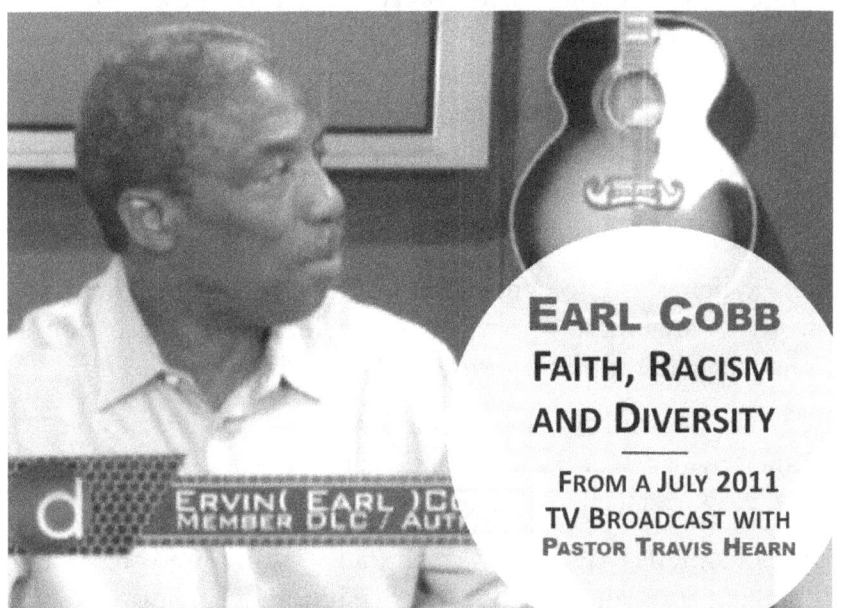

Published on February 9, 2020

While cleaning out my somewhat cramped Phoenix office this weekend, I opened a box and noticed an old DVD case titled, *Desert Life Church Scottsdale, Arizona TV Broadcast July 17, 2011 (James 2:4)*.

I opened the case and found that the DVD contained a copy of the actual interview I gave almost ten years ago while attending a church in North Scottsdale. The church has since changed its name to Impact Church. At the time, the Senior Pastor, Travis Hearn, wanted to have a discussion with me on the topic of "Racism and Discrimination".

The interview was to air on the Church's weekly Sunday night TV program following a sermon Pastor Travis (as everyone calls him) wanted to preach on the messages he finds in his understanding of James 2:4.

This morning I attended a local church in downtown Phoenix where the pastor preached a sermon based on a text from the book of Exodus. The bible story goes as follows: God told Moses (one of His high performers) to "go forward" and "trust me" and be assured that I will make a clear path by "parting" the Red Sea. Because God knew that Moses, and the people following him, would not meet their destiny if they just "parked there".

When I listened and watched the interview for the first time in over nine years, I noticed how relevant the discussion still is relative to the topics of *racism* and *diversity* in our country.

To be truthful, I was surprised at how I was able to "so concisely" answer the relative difficult questions I was asked.

In addition, since I am now about 10 years from having the responsibilities of leading technology teams and 10 years into thinking innovatively about leadership and helping to develop a new generation of leaders, this morning's sermon helped me in two interesting ways.

Firstly, it gave me a new way to think about the two most difficult obstacles that most of my clients face in their effort to become better leaders within their organization --- "comfort" and "change".

Secondly, this morning's sermon reinforced my deep understanding of the most important relationship today's senior leaders can develop with those that they lead---if they really desire to keep them "moving forward" and becoming future leaders.

The relationship is one based on "mutual trust".

For today's senior leaders to reach their own maximum level of success [personally and organizationally], they must work hard at building genuinely "trustworthy" and "faithful" relationships with all of those they lead.

My extensive research and real-world experience indicate that such relationships within any workplace can help "high-performers" more easily breakthrough today's comforts, reduce the fears of change and realize that they must move forward --- and not just "park there".

"The ability to professionally and productively address organizational conflict is an important and critical area of leadership competency."

Resolve to Better Manage Conflict within Your Organization and Your Life

Published on January 2, 2020

For many reasons most supervisors, managers and project leaders tend to continue to struggle when it comes to winning the battle of conflict avoidance.

The ability to professionally deal with organizational conflict is an important and critical area of leadership competency.

Conflict avoidance is prevalent within all organizational structures. Even among outstanding managers, supervisors, and project leaders there is a natural tendency to rationalize the need to confront conflict. Thus, the conflict continues to impact organizational performance, customer satisfaction and career promotion opportunities.

"How" to fortify foundational and emotional shortcomings in this area will vary based on your inherit strengths, weaknesses and abilities to enable the personal and professional changes required.

However, I suggest that you "test drive" some of the following techniques.

1. Express your contrary opinion as an "and."

Keep in mind that it is not necessary for someone else to be wrong for you to be right.

2. Use hypotheticals.

If you do not feel comfortable being assertive when addressing a co-worker or superior, then ask them to imagine a different scenario.

3. Discuss the perceived impact of the action.

Instead of simply disagreeing with the action, help others think through the consequences by asking good open-ended questions about the potential impact.

4. Ask about the underlying issue.

If you disagree, start the discussion by trying to clarify and understand the other person's rationale. If you understand the reason for the action, you might be able to mutually find another way to accomplish the same goal.

LEADERSHIP FRONT AND CENTER

FOUR OF MY BIGGEST LESSONS LEARNED IN 2019

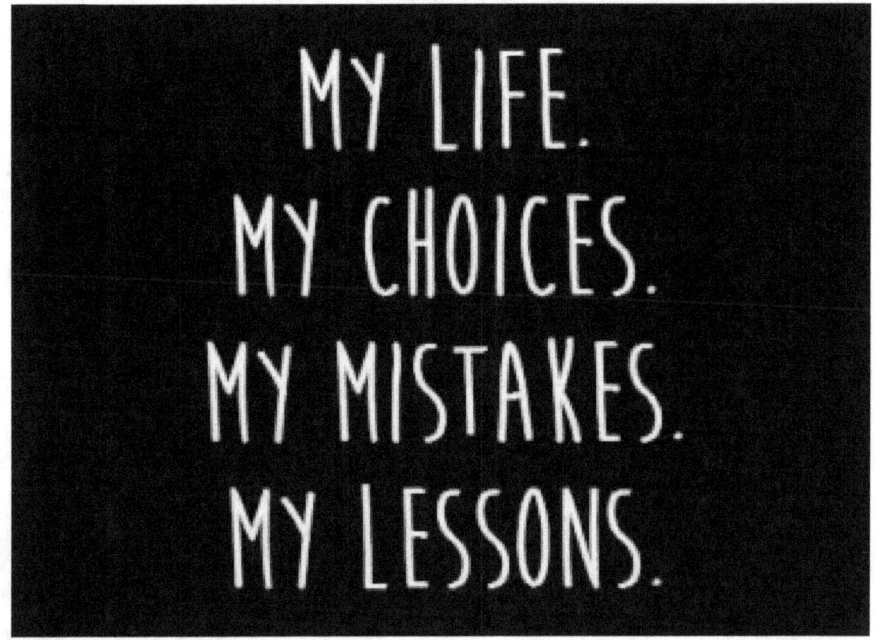

Published on December 22, 2019

It is hard to believe, but 2019 has almost come to a close. Since at Richer Life, LLC our motto is "Shaping Thoughts and Changing Lives for the Better," I want our authors and faithful followers to learn from our successes and challenges in 2019.

So, here are the biggest publishing "lessons learned" that our RICHER Press publishing team learned in 2019. I believe that they are also "lessons learned" that may help you achieve goals in both your professional and personal life in 2020.

1. TO BE PATIENT

We do not need everything to happen at once. We also do not need to publish a large number of books every year.

However, we do need to make sure

that we are here year-after-year to support our published authors. This support includes book promotions, book sales, author royalty tracking, royalty payments and hopefully, for time-to-time, assisting them with writing and publishing another book.

There is a lot of waiting in the niche publishing business. Waiting for a manuscript to be finished, waiting for the illustrator to finish the art, waiting to design each page, waiting for the printer to print the book, waiting for the books to be shipped to our distributors and waiting to see if an authors' book sells and is well-received.

Therefore, we have learned to take a breath and be patient.

2. GO DIRECT TO POTENTIAL CONSUMERS AND READERS

As a niche publisher, our ability to be nimble, quick to market, savvy, and innovative allows us to take advantage of all the unpredictable and sometimes erratic ways that direct-to-consumer can manifest.

One example here is to encourage our RICHER Press authors who are only selling a few books a year to work with local non-profit and fundraising organizations. Under RICHER Press publishing guidelines, these organizations can buy books directly from the author at near-wholesale cost. This allows the fundraising organizations to offer the books at an increased cost to raise funds. For the "right" organizations, it can beat selling cookies or chicken dinners.

Because buyers are already supporters of the organization, many will simply buy the books to show or continue their support. This enables this approach to generate more funds more quickly. While at the same time, the fundraising organizations contribute to the overall literacy of their communities as well as seed opportunities to increase the author's readership and future book sales.

3. CONTINUE TO PROMOTE ALL TITLES

One of the great benefits that RICHER Press receives by being a member of the IBPA (Independent Book Publishers Association) is having a chance to participate in various marketing programs.

In 2019 RICHER Press participated in a program which took a book published back in 2015 and targeted a series of blogs which needed content on a specific topic. We were delighted to see that because of the e-blast we sent out, the author landed an interview on a podcast (one that is perfectly aligned with the messages in the book) and increased his annual book sales through our distribution channels.

Oftentimes, we focus so much of our marketing strategy on the launch of a new book and then a year later we quickly move on to the next project. But, we have learned that it can be beneficial to continue to promote all RICHER Press titles where the authors are still interested in increasing readership and, more importantly, where the authors are actively involved in promoting their published work. We have learned that readers of all book genres just want to read good books and they do not care when they were published.

5. TRY NEW BUSINESS INITIATIVES, PRACTICES AND RELATIONSHIPS.

In 2019, we tried a few new business initiatives, practices and relationships in an effort to grow, but found that several of these efforts were non-starters, leaving us short of our publishing goals for

the year. We were more focused on business performance than on the business essentials.
Sometimes you can work so hard at something that you veer off-course.

Going too fast and ignoring the signs of trouble ahead is exactly what sunk the Titanic! This year we turned our ship around by completing some key infrastructure improvements and building upon some great author and distribution relationships.

As a result, in 2019 we will end the year selling more children's books and selling into more international markets than any time in our 10-year history.

I wish you a safe and enjoyable Holiday Season and a most prosperous New Year!

LEADERSHIP FRONT AND CENTER

HOW PREPARED ARE YOU TO PROTECT YOURSELF AND DO YOUR JOB TODAY?

Published on May 22, 2020

I am proud of myself for continuing my daily exercise routine far beyond middle age. In today's business environment, both good physical and mental health is required to sustain focus and to remain competitive in any profession.

One morning last week after completing my workout, I walked into the men's locker room and noticed a man who was also a regular club member. He was in the process of changing into his work attire.

During the six months I have worked out at this particular facility, I have been impressed with how hard this person worked out at 5:00 AM in the morning. I could see in the level of determination given each exercise routine that he was a person with a professional mission in life.

As I sit down on a bench across the room from him and without staring, I suddenly could not resist observing how methodically and consciously he was putting on his outfit and the "gear" required for him to be "prepared" to protect himself and to "do his job well."

After putting on his shoes and uniform, there was the leather belt and the duty holster. Then, also around his waist, he put on the flashlight holder, the glove holder, the handcuff holder, the key holder, the baton holder, the defense spray holder, the magazine holder, the phone holder and the two-way radio holder.

Following the placement of the flashlight, gloves, handcuffs, keys, baton, defense spray and magazine of ammunition in their respective locations, he carefully holstered his radio and service revolver prior to slipping on his bulletproof vest.

As he picked up his gym bag and walked out the door, I began to think about not just the "gear" he had to carry around all day, but also the physical strength, the mental alertness and the courage required for law enforcement professionals to be prepared to maintain order, protect us as citizens and potentially engage in life-threatening conflict.

Just like all *high performing* professionals, law enforcement officers must also be prepared to make split-second decisions that may be ethically & legally complex and may call for advanced tactics and team coordination. Adequate physical and mental preparation in all aspects of any profession is necessary to effectively get the job done.

As I sat down at my desk cuddling my third cup of coffee later that day, I could not stop thinking about the police officer --- and what I had observed while at the gym that morning.

In retrospect, I asked myself, *"How prepared am I to protect my career and do my job well every day?"* and *"Have I methodically and consciously put on all of the "gear" required to be effective in my role?"*

Fortunately, the "gear" that most organizational managers and leaders must put on each day does not include handcuffs or bulletproof vests. However, the "management and leadership gear" that is required for us to be prepared to "do our job well" is just as important for both job protection and job performance.

Surprisingly, too many organizational professionals are not aware of the fact that the management and leadership "gear" essential to their protection and performance consist of attributes and skills which are the by-products of valuing post-graduate education, professional development and skills training…the lack of which…constitutes the "trappings" which derail the full potential of many very competent professionals.

The chart below contains a set of 14 essential attributes and skills required for all professionals in today's work environment who desire to "reach" and "remain" at the top of their game.

DRIVE	SELF-RELIANCE	WILLPOWER	PATIENCE	INTEGRITY	EMPATHY	SELF-CONFIDENCE
PASSION	CONNECTION	OPTIMISM	COMMUNICATION SKILLS	PROJECT MTG SKILLS	LEADERSHIP SKILLS	TIME MANAGEMENT SKILLS

How much of this "gear" did you walk into your office with this morning?

How prepared are you to protect yourself and do your job today?

"Too many good supervisors and managers fail to achieve their full potential and miss great job and career growth opportunities.."

LEADERSHIP FRONT AND CENTER

SKINNY PRINCIPLE #1 - IT DOES MATTER

Published on November 21, 2019

Too many good supervisors and managers fail to achieve their full potential and miss great job and career growth opportunities because of five fundamental shortcomings:

1. They fail to take the time and make the effort necessary to understand the essential differences in their roles of both managing and leading within an organizational structure.

2. They fail to appreciate and prepare themselves with the leadership development training and insights vital to be successful in new leadership roles accepted within their organizations... new roles may require new skills.

3. They fail to create a clear and concise mental picture of what is required of themselves and their team members to meet the organization's expectations and ensure a "win."

4. They fail to document and effectively communicate their vision and expectations to their work teams and to all stakeholders within the organization; and

5. They fail to build and maintain the relationships needed within their teams, and the organization as a whole, in order to establish the level of respect and trust the job demands.

6. However, overcoming these shortcomings is very much in the reach of most supervisors and managers. It only requires the commitment of the time, focus and energy necessary to take the leadership strengthening actions required to be in a position to always lead and win.

Skinny Principle #1 - It Does Matter

This Principle draws attention to the fundamental truth that your roles as the "Leader" and the "Manager" are two of the most critical roles within any organization. You can either strengthen or weaken the organization's chances for success. This Principle underscores the reality that while both roles are important, your role as the organization's "Leader" differs in approach, tone, and expectations from your role as the organization's "Manager." Your ability to maintain the proper mindset, preparation and focus in each role can be the difference between winning and failing. The simplest way to think of what to keep in mind here is "I should manage tasks, assets and deadlines and I should lead people, expectations and outcomes."

LEADERSHIP FRONT AND CENTER

WHAT IS THE MOST IMPORTANT "C" WITHIN YOUR ORGANIZATION?

Published on October 29, 2019

I was asked this question a few years ago while participating on an executive panel during a professional development seminar.

My response was somewhat surprising to the audience and some other panel members.

I shared with the group the following:

I strongly believe, based on my decades of experience leading large and small companies, that any organization would greatly benefit from changes in outdated business processes and operational strategies if the word "Chief" (and its allusions) in all senior management titles was changed to "Courageous".

Why do I believe that a *"Courageous Executive Officer"* or a *"Courageous Information Officer"* would contribute more to any organization's operational success?

Here is my reasoning.

In addition to *caring* - *courage* is the only other "character" attribute required in almost every basic human activity or endeavor to successfully effect transformational change. A senior manager's success in effecting impactful change in business process and operational strategy depends heavily on her or his ability to ration individual courage consistent with the expected results.

Courage in our daily lives can sometimes be a matter of life and death. In some occupations, like being a police officer or firefighter, you are expected to routinely take courageous actions to abate danger or change behaviors that could lead to disaster. The courage in these occupations seems to be instinctive and reactionary.

However, there have been many studies on human behavior within organizations and they all seem to indicate that individual courage within companies seldom operates like this.

Leaders who act courageously, whether on behalf of society, their companies, their colleagues or their own career rarely do it impulsively. Nor does it emerge from nowhere.

In business organizations, courageous action is really a special kind of "calculated risk taking." Those of us who become good leaders have a greater than average willingness to make bold moves, but we strengthen our chances of success—and avoid career suicide—through careful deliberation and preparation.

Business courage is not so much a visionary leader's inborn characteristic as it is a skill acquired through decision-making processes that improves with practice. In other words, to maximize your ability to successfully harness and ration the courage required to effect much needed change, you must learn how to make high-risk decisions. Much of the ability to be a truly courageous leader is learned and courageous leadership blossoms over time.

As Mark Twain once wrote, *"Courage is not the absence of fear, but its mastery."* Mastering the concept of courageous leadership and taking intelligent risks requires an understanding of what I call "Calculated Risk and Reward."

Calculated Risk and Reward is a straightforward approach of making leadership success more likely while avoiding impulsive, unproductive or irrational behavior...and this includes "doing nothing."

In business organizations, as in life, taking positive, calculated risks is sometimes necessary in order to achieve an elusive goal or the next level of performance. As with any risk, there is always something at stake. In most instances, when it comes to leadership decisions, you stand to lose money, time, respect and your reputation...that are also the very same things you stand to gain.

Significantly greater than just being a *Chief*, are the rewards of having an appropriate level of disciplined *Courage*. Taking the calculated and required risks today could enrich your organization, your career and your life in the future.

"We all will miss Ann. However, I am sure that everyone she touched will benefit from her legacy."

LEADERSHIP FRONT AND CENTER

The Great Mystery Awaits Us All

Published on July 21, 2019

Every month brings something new in both our professional and personal lives. It could be a new job, a new level of responsibility or a new friend.

The first day of this month brought the news that a dear associate and friend has completed her life's journey and entered into what she so affectionately called in her only published novel "the great mystery."

I first met Ann in 2014 when her daughter, Stacey Kramer, introduced us.

Therefore, I missed being a part of the vast majority of her life. It was a vibrant life, which included a loving husband and family, becoming one of the first women in the Chicago area to lead a commercial real estate firm when she founded Ann Anovitz Associates in 1982, and an active retirement, which included volunteering and working on her art.

However, between 2014 and her passing, both I and the entire RICHER Press Publishing and author team were blessed to have had the opportunity to work with Ann and admire her energy and love of life.

During that period, Ann published four beautifully written and illustrated children's books. The unique books included both English and Spanish text designed to help young minds explore the wonders of the Sonoran Desert. They also helped them learn the importance of being a "good person" in all aspects of their lives.

Ann also worked diligently on and published a young adult novel titled *Charlie's Tale: The Great Mystery*. The book takes her readers on a "probable" after life journey to discover how the legacy of our lives on earth may affect the lives of the family members we leave behind - and affect society, as a whole.

We all will miss Ann. However, I am sure that everyone she touched will benefit from her legacy.

There is one thing that being around her, for even a short time, taught me and continues to drive my actions and attitude every day. That is, I always keep in mind that, without doubt (every day, every month and every year) will bring something new...and it is how I embrace the "newness" that will determine the impact it will have on my life.

Ann, since it has been only about 20 days since you have passed over, I know that you are at this point deeply involved in your afterlife journey. Here is to your success in finally solving *The Great Mystery*.

LEADERSHIP FRONT AND CENTER

LEADERSHIP IS SO MISUNDERSTOOD

Published on June 25, 2019

After more than three decades of working as senior leaders in corporate, within governmental organizations and a decade of researching and writing about leading within organizational structures, my wife, Dr. Charlotte Grant-Cobb and I have come to the growing realization that:

> *"What's required for a good Manager or Supervisor to become an effective leader within any organization is so misunderstood."*

Therefore, a few years ago, we decided to write this book.

Without doubt, there are many schools of thought regarding what it takes to become an "effective leader" in the 21st century. However, undeniably, being an effective leader within any organizational structure does and has always required one crucial skill: ---*The ability to influence social behavior in a manner, which maximizes the efforts of others, towards the achievement of a common goal."*

The power and effectiveness of this **crucial skill** — as personally observed and studied over the past ten years in our coaching and consulting engagements and by thousands of other experts in the field — builds a strong case in support of the following *fundamental truth:*

"It does not require special talents, advanced degrees or years of leadership experience for good managers and supervisors to become effective organizational leaders."

This *fundamental truth* supports the fact that it only requires the mastering of a proven and straightforward method of social influence in the workplace. A method which focuses on maximizing the human traits that can naturally propel any professional to become h consistently **S**tudious, **M**asterful, **A**rticulate, **R**esourceful and Trustworthy — or to become consistently **SMART** — the five attributes that are fundamental to effective organizational leadership

Based on the feedback we have received from training and career specialist, we believe that *The SMART Leader and the "Skinny" Principles* offers one of the strongest and most contemporary approaches to real-world leadership development for managers, supervisors and their organizations available anywhere today.

The SMART Leader utilizes the power of *Narrative Enhanced Leadership Development* — a learning and knowledge retention technique, which activates the brain of readers by turning stories and situational narratives into their own experiences. A compelling and suspenseful and candid *situational narrative* introduces each chapter of the book. Each narrative is written to "cut to the chase" and help the reader instantly benefit from the suggestions and guidance provided in the discussion of each "Skinny" Principle.

In ten short chapters, **The SMART Leader** presents a unique and powerful chain of reasoning, which has unquestionably guided leaders within all types of public and private organizations to phenomenal personal and professional success.

LEADERSHIP FRONT AND CENTER

WHY LIVING A RICHER LIFE IS LESS MYSTERY AND MORE MASTERY

Published on September 26, 2018

Earlier this week while reviewing my schedule for the remainder of the year, I noticed an interview on my calendar as a guest on the Conscious PIVOT Podcast. Adam Markel, best-selling author of and host of the Podcast *"PIVOT: The Art and Science of Reinventing Your Career and Life"* and the #1 Wall Street Journal Bestseller and a USA Today Bestseller, *"Soul over Matter."* Adam is a recognized expert in professional & personal reinvention and a highly sought-after public speaker, transformational leader and business mentor.

As I began to ponder the upcoming interview with Adam and his extraordinary work, vivid memories of a transformative journey my wife and I made a few years ago came to mind.

The journey involved both of us reflecting upon the many times we have "pivoted" and "re-invented" ourselves and our careers during more than three decades of marriage and life together. The unexpected and surprising length of this intellectual journey give rise to a healthy manuscript and the eventual publishing of our first book together titled, *Living a Richer Life: Getting the Most out of Life's Gifts and Circumstances.*

"Living a Richer Life" was first published in 2010. Over the years, most readers have quickly grasped the message embedded in the title and found it less of a mystery and more of an opportunity to learn how to master the art of finding more happiness in their lives.

During our journey of self-enlightenment, we discovered and coined our own definition of living a *"Richer Life."* In the book, we define a *"Richer Life"* as <u>not</u> a life filled with monetary wealth but "a life full of <u>*good decisions, financial security, great relationships, loving family memories* and a *feeling of completeness.*</u>" We called these the five *essential elements* of a happy life.

In our literary research and personal reflections, we determined that each of these five *elements* contributes equally to our ability to live a truly "richer" life. Based on the daily demands and rapidly changing challenges of life thus far in the 21st century and recent surveys, most people do agree that financial security is important, but happiness and not money is the ultimate currency in life.

However, for me, like most working people and entrepreneurs today, staying "on-track" and even getting close to mastering fulfillment in all five *elements* is quite the challenge.

I have found that the "key" lies in our *capacity* to increase our *mindfulness* and expand our *curiosity* in to create ways and opportunities to make the *appropriate adjustments* in both our professional and personal lives. Most of the time (as determined by Adam Markel in his work) making small adjustments or "pivots" can reap significant rewards.

I have included below a copy of a little "mind-juggler" or "mindfulness exercise" that I have devised to help me stay on-track and to "master" the art of reaping all of the "richness" that my life has to offer.

Even at this stage of my career and life, I still diligently find a quiet place to sit down and reflect on each of the 15 questions at least once a month. The goal is to be honest with myself and to consciously strive toward making the required adjustments or "pivots" in my monthly activities to reach maximum fulfillment in *all five elements*.

Living a Richer Life
MONTHLY MINDFULNESS CHECK-IN

GOOD DECISIONS	How many major decisions (at Work or Home) have I made this month?	In hindsight, how many of the decisions were Good Decisions and Why?	What did I learn about my decision making process that I will add to my "Decision Making Tool Kit"?
FINANCIAL SECURITY	Does my current monthly cash flow <u>exceed</u> what I need to maintain my current Financial Plan?	If, YES...Do I need to update my plan (Investments and/or Savings) to take advantage of my current earnings level and opportunities?	If, NO...What do I <u>need to do</u> or <u>can do</u> at this time to create some "cushion" to ensure I can maintain my current Financial Plan?
GREAT RELATIONSHIPS	How many of my current relationships (Personal and Professional) I would "label" as Great and why?	Do I have the opportunity at this time to improve a relationship or develop a new, beneficial relationship?	How will I approach improving current and acquiring new relationships next month?
LOVING FAMILY MEMORIES	How many new, loving family memories have I made this month...and if none...Why?	What can I change in my current routine to help create new, loving family memories "next month"?	What can I change in my current routine to help create new, loving family memories "next year"?
A FEELING OF COMPLETENESS	On a scale of 1 to 10...How do I feel about the level of Completeness in my life at this time?	If less that 10...What is missing in my life and Why?	What can I do <u>next month</u> and <u>next year</u> to maintain or move closer to feeling like a 10?

I invite you to *give it a try* for a couple of months.

Then, get back and let me know if it has helped you reap more of the *"richness"* you deserve into your life.

"*NEL works because, as humans, we are all wired to allow good stories to place us in someone else's shoes.*"

Is Narrative Enhanced Leadership What You Have Been Looking For?

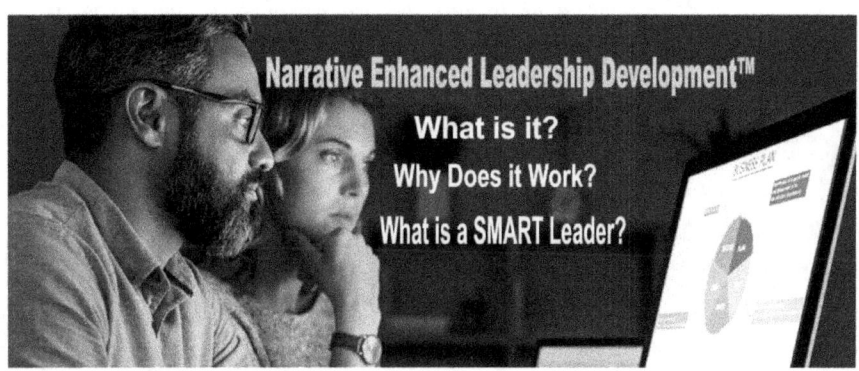

Published on April 19, 2019

For many years, researchers around the world have discovered the prevailing effect of a good story. A good story or well-written narrative can have a powerful effect on the human brain, and not just in terms of entertainment. It is no surprise that respected educational organizations are beginning to deliberately integrate storytelling into their programs and courses. Among them are Narrative 4, StoryCorps, The Kitchen Sisters and the Humans of New York.

WHAT IS IT?

Narrative Enhanced Leadership Development™ or **NEL** is a learning and knowledge retention technique specifically developed for Managers and Supervisors seeking to expand their leadership skills and career opportunities. NEL is designed to activate the brain of readers to turn *situational narratives* into their own experiences.

WHY DOES IT WORK?

A well-written narrative can help us to learn and retain important information, both in casual and formal learning settings. According to Gerry Beamish, a UK consultant who researches the value of storytelling in accelerating learning, **"A story is the only way to activate parts in the brain so that a listener turns the narrative into their own ideas and experience."**

According to Paul Zak, Director of the Center for Neuroeconomics Studies at Claremont Graduate University, *"stories capture our attention better than other information because they leave a physical and emotional trace in the brain."* Zak writes, *"As social creatures who regularly affiliate with strangers, stories are an effective way to transmit important information and values from one individual or community to the next. Stories that are personal and emotionally compelling engage more of the brain, and thus are better remembered, than simply stating a set of facts."*

Thus, NEL works because, as humans, we are all wired to allow good stories to place us in someone else's shoes – one of the best ways to appreciate and understand the hard-core realities associated with being a leader.

WHAT IS A SMART LEADER?

The reference here is to the archetype of The SMART Leader as set forth in the new book, *The Smart Leader and the "Skinny" Principles: How to Lead and Win within Any Organization* by Ervin (Earl) Cobb and Charlotte D. Grant-Cobb, PhD. Earl and Charlotte are the authors of ten published books. Their published work is highly respected for being ultra-contemporary and even life changing.

The break-through book, released in the fall of 2019, builds upon a carefully chosen collection of what is called *"Skinny" Principles.* These Principles candidly "cut to the chase" and simplify what must be done to address the hard-core realities embedded within the challenging art of leading within 21st century organizations. In ten short chapters, the reader is provided the What, Why, How and When associated with mastering the "Skinny" Principles.

Each chapter is introduced by an ultra-contemporary and suspenseful situational narrative written to help guide Managers and Supervisors tackle the leadership challenges they are faced with today or will face in the future. The print book includes coaching tools and exercises.

LEADERSHIP FRONT AND CENTER

THE NEED TO ELEVATE YOUR GAME IN ORDER TO MOVE TO AND SUCCEED AT THE NEXT LEVEL

Published on February 6, 2019

While working longer hours and taking on more responsibility in your current job may seem to be the right thing to do in order to move to that next level, it was rarely sufficient during the course of my career and is even less sufficient in today's work environment. Successful career mobility is anchored around your ability to elevate your game and to take advantage of opportunities that surface beyond what you are doing today.

I recall being asked by a corporate board member to move from my role as Chief Operating Officer to the role of CEO of a venture-backed high-tech company that I had joined only a year prior. I immediately realized that I would have to elevate my game and begin to think like the CEO and to do the things a CEO would do on a daily basis as compared to my previous role. Since the opportunity surfaced later in my career, I was equipped with the skills and the emotional intelligence to make this kind of pivot.

But, regardless of the stage of your professional career, when you have a need to move to the next level of job performance or to the next job, having an answer to these three questions can be paramount to successfully reaching your goal:

1). Are my thoughts consistent with what will be required in the new role?

2). Do I have a platform of activities/actions that, if executed, will ensure a successful transition? And

3.) Do I have a method of tracking my progress from start to success?

Personal Adage:

Once you have the degrees and the credentials, your thoughts are key to increasing your leadership influence and accelerating your career growth regardless of your profession.

While working longer hours and taking on more responsibility in your current job may seem to be the right thing to do in order to move to that next level, it was rarely sufficient during the course of my career and is even less sufficient in today's work environment.

Successful career mobility is anchored around your ability to elevate your game and to take advantage of opportunities that surface beyond what you are doing today.

THE MOTHER OF ALL HOLIDAY WISHES

Published on December 21, 2018

This year I celebrated my 65th birthday. Like many of you, over the years I have received hundreds of holiday greetings and well wishes. Most have wished me a Merry Christmas, a Happy Holiday and a Happy New Year.

As we approach the pinnacle of this year's holiday season, I am sure that you have received and have given many holiday wishes.

However, have you taken the time to think about the answer to this question: "What would be the best wish that you could give to anyone during the holiday season or at any time during the year?"

In other words, "What would be the Mother of all wishes?"

Well, the answer to this question has constantly been on my mind since I returned last week from a visit with my sister in Florida.

She recently celebrated her 76th birthday and a few years ago, she was diagnosed with dementia. This progressive and sometimes chronic brain condition causes problems with thinking, behavior, and memory.

During my four-hour flight home, I reflected on her condition and the time I had just spent with her. As I thought through my recent visit with her, I could not help saying to myself, "I wish she was better". Yet, in hindsight, "better" is not what I really wished since better simply implies an improvement in her condition.

As I thought deeper through the details of my conversations with her and my observations of her behavior, it became more obvious that "getting better" was not what she was wishing for either. It finally sunk in. Even though I may not have fully accepted her chronic condition... she has.

Now, I realize that the random verbal expressions, her physical uneasiness and the inquisitiveness of her eyes all indicated that what she was wishing to find was some "peace."

I believe that as we all go through our daily routines, our ability to cope and succeed is heavily dependent on us knowing that we are in control of our mind, that we know what is in our heart and that we know that all is well.

Therefore, on behalf of all of us here at Richer Life, LLC, I extend to all of you this holiday season, the Mother of all wishes --- Peace of Mind, Peace of Heart and Peace of Well-Being.

LEADERSHIP FRONT AND CENTER
BELIEVE IT OR NOT - THIS IS WHY PROJECT MANAGERS ARE BECOMING LEADERS

Published on July 27, 2018

Too many Project Managers are falling short when it comes to their leadership responsibilities. A sincere focus on their own Leadership Development can reap professional and financial rewards.

Despite the significant technical advancements in the Project Management Profession, research studies still show an increase in project failures globally, emphasizing the importance of the Project Manager's role as a *"Leader."*

Although there are extensive course offerings for Project Management training, the global offering of real-world and effective leadership development for Project Managers has been slow to emerge.

Most training programs today target the *"neocortex"*. The neocortex is the part of the brain that is traditionally associated with learning and thinking. This type of training is appropriate if the desired outcome is the memorization of facts to pass a test. However, contemporary research shows that if the objective is to transform a Project Manager, from the inside, into a *"Leader,"* the target must be the *"limbic"* portion of the brain, which is associated with feelings and emotions.

Essential to a *"limbic-focused"* approach to leadership development is the ability to take the learner to a place where he or she can do the following:

(1) Emotionally, as well as methodically, think through the difference between being a *"Leader"* versus just a "Manager" in the most challenging workplace situations.

(2) Intellectually embrace and accomplish the professional and personal tasks required to successfully complete a genuine transformation from *"Manager"* to *"Leader";* and

(3) Recognize that, with the proper focus, commitment and support, it is possible to make this transformation irrespective of prior leadership background and career stage.

Years of experience has shown that the goal of gaining forward-thinking leadership skills and making the psychological changes vital to becoming an effective *"Leader"* is in the reach of most Project Managers.

This practical and life-changing journey is indeed a transformation of how a Project Manager thinks about and executes leadership responsibilities. If properly constructed, the journey can be fun, insightful, and inspiring.

Possessing the ability to *"think like and generate the results of a Leader"* is a highly valued professional asset and can positively change the trajectory of any manager's career.

Why More Project Managers are Becoming Project Leaders

Published on July 12, 2018

In December 2015, the Project Management Institute (PMI®) updated its Continuing Certification Requirements (CCR) Program to include a Talent Triangle concept. According to the PMI, "The ideal [PM] skill set is a combination of technical, leadership, and strategic and business management expertise." Prior to this update, project leadership was not a major component of formal Project Management training.

Data: 2017 PayScale, Inc.

Being recognized as a Project Leader and not just a Project Manager not only comes with skills that are in high demand globally but also with more career opportunities and higher salaries.

For many Project Management Professionals (PMP®) and Functional Managers who have various Project Management responsibilities, a self-directed leadership development program is the best and most effective approach.

The Self-Directed Leadership Development option allows these professionals to confront their own internal ideas, preconceptions, and thinking patterns; determine their individual leadership and career development needs; and craft an executable action plan that will successfully move them from Project Manager to Project Leader. All is accomplished at a pace which best fit their current professional and personal situation.

In January 2017, Jim Grigsby and I completed a lengthy period of research which included literature analysis, surveys, workshops and focus groups.

As we reflected upon all of the documentation from our research and our own career experiences, we decided to spend the next year developing a comprehensive workbook and coaching guide that could be used by those PMP professionals, Program/Project Managers and Functional Business Managers.

This is a group who could significantly benefit from transforming from *"good manager"* to *"outstanding leader"* - at a pace which best fit their current professional and personal situation.

We are happy to announce that our work was published in March 2018 as a new, 240-page book titled, *"Driving Ultimate Project Performance: Transforming from Project Manager to Project Leader."*

The comprehensive Workbook and Coaching Guide is designed to be effectively used independently or with the assistance of a Development Coach. The goal to provide a proven framework to allow PMPs, Program/Project Managers and Functional Business Managers to learn about their Leadership style, strengthen their Leadership skills, build a solid foundation for their Leadership transformation and become the outstanding leaders they desire to be.

The book is uniquely written to provide the professional guidance and insight throughout the transformation process.

I invite you to take a serious look at the book and imagine how you would be better equipped for your next project assignment if you took the time to complete this type of high caliber, professional development exercise.

I hope that some of you will take advantage of this exclusive, Linked In opportunity to build a more fulfilling personal and professional life.

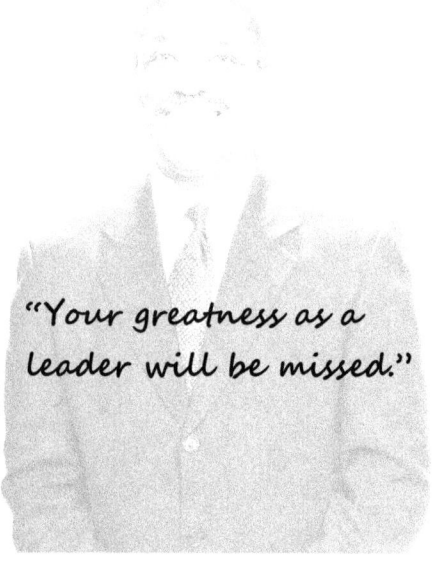

"Your greatness as a leader will be missed."

LEADERSHIP FRONT AND CENTER

When They Feel Your Presence in Your Absence - You Have Led

Published on January 22, 2018

It's hard for me to believe that August of this year will mark the 43rd anniversary of the start of my career as a technologist, corporate vice president, entrepreneur and avid student of organizational leadership. After spending over 20 years leading corporate organizations and publishing three books on leadership development, I thought that I had "broken the code" and knew almost everything there is to know "about how to determine if you are a great leader - until yesterday.

First, here is a little background.

After graduating from engineering school in 1975, I started my career working for Honeywell, Inc. in Phoenix, Arizona. I can vividly recall what it was like being a "twenty-something" in Phoenix in the 1970's. Much of the community activity at that time for most African American professionals, like me, was about "change."

From marching to gain support of a MLK day in Arizona to creating opportunities for networking for Black professionals, it was a time of both professional and personal growth. Having grown up in church as a youth, I shortly became affiliated with a small, inner-city Phoenix church with around 200 members, named the Pilgrim Rest Baptist Church.

During my time at Pilgrim Rest Baptist Church in the late 1970's, I was asked to teach a youth Sunday school class. All the students in the class seemed eager to learn about the gospel. But there was one 9-year-old young man who stood out from the others. He would be dressed on Sunday mornings in a black suit, white shirt, black tie and always with a small black fedora on his head. I remember saying to myself, "this young man is not only dressing differently, and he also seems to be very confident in where he is headed."

I later learned that he had been ordained as a Minister at age seven. Before I left the Phoenix area in 1986, he had already become the youngest Pastor of Pilgrim Rest Baptist Church (at age sixteen) and was beginning to expand the church and grow the congregation.

Now, let us go back to me thinking that I knew everything "about how you can determine if you are a great leader" and "yesterday".

Yesterday, my wife and I sat among a congregation in a mega-church in downtown Phoenix with over 4,000 members. As you might have guessed, the church was the now expanded Pilgrim Rest Baptist Church. Over a thirty-year period, the church's Senior Pastor, Bishop Alexis Thomas (the nine-year-old from my Sunday school class back in 1977), had realized his vision. From being a "child Prodigy," he had grown to become a dynamic preacher, passionate orator, and exceptional church leader.

However, yesterday was not *service as usual*. Earlier in the week the congregation had suddenly lost their leader of 33 years at age 50 and it was an unfortunate time for mourning and reflection.

As I sat in the church yesterday reflecting on my relationship with and the extraordinary life of Bishop Alexis Thomas, I looked around the huge sanctuary and saw both pain and joy on the faces of almost the entire congregation. As the service progressed, I could literally feel the heightened emotions illuminating throughout building. From the youngest to the oldest, each face of those present seemed to say that they knew exactly "why" they would personally miss him.

It seemed that some of them may have been fellow members of the clergy; some may have known him for a long time; some may have been close friends, some may have just been faithful church members; while others may have felt and benefited from the positive impact of his leadership throughout the greater Phoenix community and in all the communities that he touched across the country.

But, above all, it seemed that everyone "felt his presence in his absence."

It was at that moment I realized that what I was experiencing was the life changing power of Bishop Alexis Thomas' affectionate and tireless leadership and the positive difference it had made in the lives of so many people for such a long time.

Now I recognize that one of the most affirmative ways you can determine your "greatness" as a leader is not just by knowing that you have made everyone around you better, but also knowing that "your presence will be felt in your absence."

Job well done, Bishop Alexis Thomas.

Your greatness as a leader will be missed. But yesterday demonstrated to me that your presence is eternally in the minds and hearts of those you have touched. I believe that it will continue to make them, and future generations, better.

"Over the past 40 years both my experience and research have revealed to me Ten Absolute Attributes all closely associated with effective leaders."

A Professional and Personal Advantage You Might Be Missing and What You are Losing

Published on November 27, 2017

Have you ever thought about the advantages of leadership and being an effective leader?

Just as a verb is the most important part of completing a sentence, leadership can become the most important part of influencing the activities required to accomplish important goals in both your personal and professional life.

The most effective leaders have a distinct advantage in the ease in which they deploy their strongest leadership attributes. They seem to consistently achieve both personal and professional success. They tend to get more leadership opportunities, win more of the battles in the trenches and earn more recognition, more acknowledgment, more respect, and more rewards.

How do they do this? What comprises their primary set of leadership attributes?

Well, over the past 40 years both my experience and research have revealed to me Ten Absolute Attributes all closely associated with effective leaders. These Attributes are considered absolute because when strategically deployed they appear to be all that's required to provide them a distinct advantage over their peers.

What are these ten attributes you ask? Well, they are in the chart below:

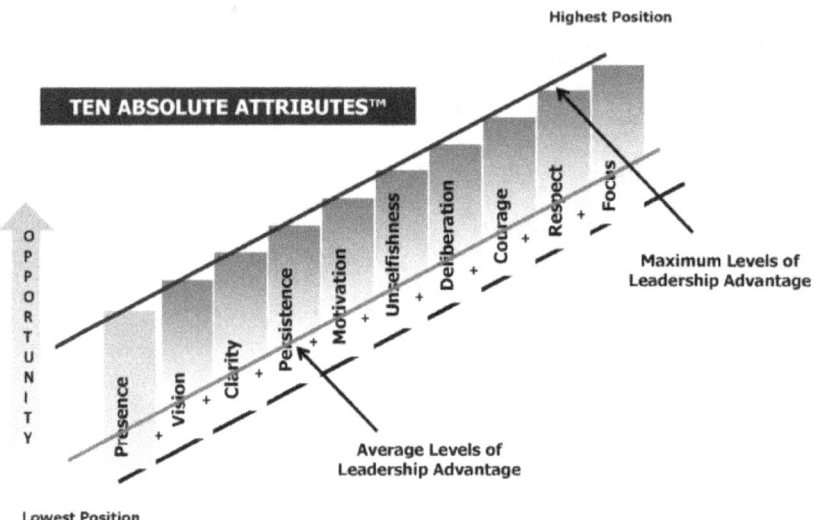

Each of these attributes encompasses an inherent human characteristic that most people possess to some extent and each embodies a distinct personal trait. However, the challenge is that each trait can also be lessened and even discounted by others if not strategically and consciously deployed.

Here are a couple of examples.

We all have some level of presence. When we walk into a room, we will be noticed. *However, do you always know by whom and to what degree?*

We all depend on a plan, a road map, or a vision to know what to do next or what to expect at the end of a journey. But, how broad and how deep is your visioning and can it be effectively communicated to others?

WHY TRADITIONAL LEADERSHIP TRAINING ROUTINELY FAIL THOSE WHO DESIRE TO BECOME OUTSTANDING PROJECT LEADERS
---PART ONE---

Published on August 20, 2017

INTRODUCTION TO THE SERIES

Since developing a profound interest in the Project Management profession during my first program/project management position with Motorola's Government and Systems Technology Group in 1979, I have been captivated by the wide-ranging impact and influence an outstanding project leader can have within a project of any type and any size.

Although, it was not until after dozens of project assignments within various industries and organizational cultures that I came to grips with the fact that "All project leaders are project managers, but not all project managers are project leaders." Throughout my corporate career, encompassing senior project management and executive roles, I have continued to observe what I now call the "Project Management vs. Project Leadership Disconnect."

In recent years, I have lectured and written extensively about the power of personal and organizational "leadership" and the advantages that outstanding leaders have over their peers in both career and personal success. My latest book focuses on the stark differences between Project Management and Project Leadership. It also provides some practical self-help tools that can aid in the challenging transformation from "project manager" to "project leader."

I was delighted when one of the most respected organizations in the project management profession, the Project Management Institute or PMI, developed and began endorsing the PMI Talent Triangle. The PMI Talent Triangle defines the ideal project management skill set as a combination of 1) technical, 2) leadership, and 3) strategic and business management expertise.

I certainly agree that the elevation of "leadership skills" to the same level as technical skills and business expertise is a big step toward pointing aspiring project managers in the right direction to become outstanding project leaders.

However, my experience as a practitioner, student and professor of leadership development has galvanized my belief that the traditional leadership skills taught in many schools and presented in most workshops "fall short", and fail those who have a desire to become outstanding project leaders. Although valuable in hierarchical organizational structures, traditional leadership skills fall short of encompassing the complete skill-set necessary for a project manager to become an outstanding project leader in a highly matrixed organizational structure.

Industry and academic experts would agree that in addition to project-specific leadership skills, outstanding project leaders in today's global, fast-paced business environment must also develop the skills needed to:

1) Visualize and manage the "big" project picture.

2) Neutralize difficult project relationships and strengthen supportive relationships.

3) Gain the trust of key shareholders and the favor of the doubters; and

4) Navigate shifting business strategies to achieve the best possible outcomes.

Acquiring such a combination of insight and intellectual prowess requires more than day-to-day project management experience and team building skills. It requires a personal acceptance of the multi-dimensional demands of outstanding project leadership, a professional commitment to one's own leadership development and a willingness to learn from the experience of those who have achieved recognition as an outstanding project leader. Finding and retaining such a "mentor" is not an easy task. However, having a professional relationship with someone who has "been there" and who has the ability to effectively share and coach, when needed, can be priceless.

In this series of articles, I will reveal and discuss a four-step process, which can propel motivated project professionals through the transformation required to become outstanding project leaders.

"I also indicated that a series of articles would follow and reveal a four-step process ...here is a brief summary of the first of the four-steps."

WHY TRADITIONAL LEADERSHIP TRAINING ROUTINELY FAIL THOSE WHO DESIRE TO BECOME OUTSTANDING PROJECT LEADERS
---PART TWO---

Published on October 20, 2017

This is the second part of a series of articles addressing the question; *"Why Traditional Leadership Training Routinely Fail Those Who Desire to Become Outstanding Project Leaders."*

In the first article, published on August 20, 2017, I shared that it was not until after dozens of project assignments within various industries and organizational cultures that I came to grips with the fact that "All project leaders are project managers, but not all project managers are project leaders."

Correspondingly, I noted that Industry and academic experts would agree that in addition to project-specific leadership skills, outstanding project leaders in today's global, fast-paced business environment must also develop the skills needed to:

1) Visualize and manage the "big" project picture.

2) Neutralize difficult project relationships and strengthen supportive relationships.

3) Gain the trust of key shareholders and the favor of the doubters; and

4) Navigate shifting business strategies to achieve the best possible outcomes.

I also indicated that a series of articles would follow and reveal a four-step process, which I believe can propel motivated project professionals through the transformation required to become outstanding project leaders.

Here is a brief summary of the first of the four-steps.

Step One: CAP-IT

Most of us can recall a moment during the execution of a challenging project when something within us kicked in and said, "It's time for me to step up and be a better project leader here." Chances are the moment resulted in you making a very difficult decision, saying "no" to an absurd request from a powerful stakeholder or persuading an executive sponsor to change project direction due to previously unknown and unsurmountable obstacles threatening to seriously affect cost and schedule.

At that time, you seem to have gone through a transformation of some sort. You suddenly had a momentary glimpse of the "bigger" picture and, at least for a moment, you felt the vibes from your project team members acknowledging an outstanding leadership performance.

Most good project managers will have good leadership moments. On occasion, they will appear to be outstanding project leaders.

However, my experience has shown me, time after time, that maintaining a consistent level of leadership consciousness require the transformation of our perspective as it relates to the role and mission of project leadership versus project management. Our perspective on any situation is governed by our thoughts. It is our thoughts that turn into actions and only timely actions generate outstanding results.

The concept of transforming from a good Project Manager to an outstanding Project Leader is a very challenging one.

Nevertheless, many project professionals do successfully achieve this accomplishment and reap the rewards associated with being outstanding project leaders.

When asked, "What had contributed most to their new leadership perspective and performance?" - most will agree that it is their newfound ability to "think like a leader."

A common and valuable stating point in such a transformation is for an aspiring project leader to create, what I call, a "transformation foundation." As with any underpinning, a transformation foundation can provide a stable and honest platform to evaluate your current leadership performance, identify your leadership development needs and determine your career advancement prospects.

I have learned over the years that only having a superficial understanding of anything that was critical to my success only leads to doubt, presumptions and the eventual failure to produce the expected outcomes. In the words of Lao Tzu, the Chinese philosopher and writer, "He who knows others is wise; he who knows himself is enlightened."

This first step of a process that I believe can propel motivated project professionals through this challenging transformation involves an approach that I have coined as CAP-IT.

When effectively executed, CAP-IT provides focused and driven project professionals a transformation foundation, which can reveal where they currently are on the Project Leadership Performance and Capability Spectrum, the heights they are capable of reaching and the best route to obtain ultimate project performance.

Here is a synopsis of what CAP-IT involves, and it can enable aspiring project leaders to CAPTURE - "their full potential."

Create a Compelling Vision of "You" – "The Outstanding Project Leader"

Before you can seriously believe in a goal or objective, you first must have an idea of what it looks like. To paraphrase the old adage: We must see it before we can believe it. Visualizing the "outstanding project leader" in you is simply a technique for creating a mental image of a future "you." When you visualize your desired outcome, you begin to "see" the possibility of achieving it. Through visualization, you catch a glimpse of what can be.

Analyze Your Current Situation and Leadership Strengths

The first step in determining where you want to be is to understand where you are. In the words of the baseball great Yogi Berra, "If you don't know where you're going, you might not get there." Knowing what you are doing or not doing today allows you to identify both strengths and weaknesses. The analysis should involve using a performance-tracking tool and keeping a record or diary to reflect an accurate picture or your reality.

Plan Your Transformation Journey

Many people who yearn for personal or professional transformation without knowing how to start such a challenging change in their lives. You can easily waste your time and energy on false starts or take a few steps in the right direction, only to find that old habits and past conditioning pull you back to where you began. Your successful journey from "project manager" to "project leader" requires a thoughtful and realistic transformation plan.

Imagine and Construct Your Transformation Support Team and Communications Strategy

It is impossible to achieve a major self-development goal without managing and getting the right level of support from all those around you. Therefore, it is important to imagine everyone you will meet during your transformation period and construct a support team and communications strategy. Not everyone you will meet will or should be on your support team. However, you must have a communication strategy, which keeps everyone informed and involved at the desired level.

Take the Actions Required to: Embrace the 7-Habits of Successful Project Leaders, Harness the Wisdom of Others and Systematically…

Execute Your Plan.

In the next article, I will reveal and discuss step two of the four-step process, *Embracing the 7-Habits of Successful Project Leaders.*

"We have all heard a form of these universal adages, "You are what you think" and "if you can't measure it, you can't change it."

LEADERSHIP FRONT AND CENTER

WHY THINKING LIKE A LEADER IS MORE THAN HALF OF THE BATTLE

Published on July 13, 2017

We have all heard a form of these universal adages, *"You are what you think"* and *"if you can't measure it, you can't change it."*

However, it wasn't until after spending thirty-four years in both the technical trenches and in the humble halls of senior management in some innovative and pioneering Fortune 500 companies - like Honeywell, Motorola, Reynolds and Reynolds and Wells Fargo Bank - that I gained a genuine respect for the roles that thinking like a leader and tracking your own on-the-job performance play in your ability to move from the cubical to the corner office.

I now know this to be true regardless of your profession, your industry, or your organizational culture. I also learned, through the school of hard knocks that by accurately digesting other's experiences and accomplishments, you can become a more thoughtful professional and propel your own career success.

In a recent conversation with a colleague, I was asked to put some meat on the bones of this idea and to provide some personal examples of why thinking like a leader and tracking your own on-the-job performance are key components for increasing leadership success in today's work place.

Well, here are three common workplace situations that helped me become more aware of the power of thinking like a leader, the value of thought guides (in person or in narrative) and the importance of tracking my on-the-job performance.

Fresh on the job with a new degree and/or certification I started my career as a member of an Advanced Engineering Program within a major mainframe computer company. The goal of the program was to accelerate the professional growth of its members and to transform successful students into successful workers.

As we all know, academic qualifications and certifications are important to be competitive in any job market. However, as I learned quickly, the ultimate key to success within any profession or organization is to become intimately aware of the standard processes, procedures and methods of operation that were in place when you arrived and will most likely be there when you leave. Then, when you master the basics, decide if you want to be a leader or a follower. If you decide to take the leadership track, there are a few things that you should do.

First, identify a few proven leaders in the organization and get close enough to them to understand how they approach their leadership roles and how they have been "taught to think." It will be quite beneficial for you to become aware of what they think about most often and why. It would also be good to know the boxes that they check within the organization to sell their ideas and the best of communication style to use (up and down the organization) to be heard.

Above all, make sure you get close enough to understand the company's scoring sheet (i.e. how you are being graded by those who matter) and make sure you keep your own score (to know where you stand). By learning to think this way, I moved from systems engineer to program manager within five years for my first college degree.

Personal Adage: The sooner you learn how to think like a successful leader and become promotion material, the sooner you will get promoted. Also, always remember, once you get near the top you are only there at the pleasure of the King…or the Queen.

The first big project within a seriously matrixed organization I was promoted to my first big project when I was 28 years old. It was within a seriously matrixed organization which was a part of a Fortune 100 multi-national company. As the project quickly morphed into a $100 million classified government contract with over 200 team members and multiple military customers, I found myself seriously in need of a leadership playbook to follow.

As an engineer, I had no problem thinking like an engineer. However, as a young project manager, I had plenty of project management skills but few of the interpersonal skills and leadership skills required to stay connected to and in control of multiple functions with competing agendas.

As a result, I was quickly overwhelmed. It was not until I was fortunate enough to find a senior mentor and guide who gave me weekly pointers as to what I should be thinking about and what I should be doing on a daily basis that I began to re-gain control. I recall taking notes during each of our weekly mentor/mentee meetings and constructing a to think about list as well as a to do and when list.

I would carry both lists with me daily to track my actual performance against my plan.

To this very day, I still begin every major project with both a think about list and a to do and when list to ensure that my thoughts, as a leader, are at the level that the tasks at hand require and that my daily performance is consistent with my plan.

Personal Adage: If I have not been there and haven't done that, I will seek out where I can quickly get a glimpse of what I need to know and go there. The need to elevate your game to move toward and succeed at the next level.

While working longer hours and taking on more responsibility in your current job may seem to be the right thing to do in order to move to that next level, it was rarely sufficient during the course of my career and is even less sufficient in today's work environment. Successful career mobility is anchored around your ability to elevate your game and to take advantage of opportunities that surface beyond what you are doing today.

I recall being asked by a corporate board member to move from my role as Chief Operating Officer to the role of CEO of a venture-backed high-tech company that I had joined only a year prior. I immediately realized that I would have to elevate my game and begin to think like the CEO and to do the things a CEO would do on a daily basis as compared to my previous role. Since the opportunity surfaced later in my career, I was equipped with the skills and the emotional intelligence to make this kind of pivot.

But, regardless of the stage of your professional career, when you have a need to move to the next level of job performance or to the next job, having a answer to these three questions can be paramount to successfully reaching your goal:

> 1). Is my trend of thought and my perspective consistent with what will be required in the new role?
>
> 2). Do I have a platform of activities/actions that, if executed, will ensure a successful transition? And

3.) Do I have a method of tracking my progress from start to success?

Personal Adage: Once you have the degrees and the credentials, your thoughts are key to increasing your leadership influence and accelerating your career growth regardless of your profession.

ABOUT THE AUTHOR

Ervin (Earl) Cobb

Over the past decade, Earl has been a powerful voice and passionate thought leader. His written work, presentations and coaching has provided thousands of organizational managers and those in leadership roles the guidance and insight required to close leadership skills gaps and become highly effective leaders. Earl has written and published more than fifty books and articles that have reached and contributed to the leadership development of professionals around the globe.

Earl is an accomplished corporate executive, leadership coach, lecturer, and entrepreneur. He is currently the CEO & Managing Partner of Richer Life, LLC.

Earl has held senior technical and leadership positions within Fortune 100, Mid-market and Venture companies including *Honeywell, Inc., Motorola, Inc., The Reynolds and Reynolds Company* and *Wells Fargo Bank*. He is the former President, COO and CEO of the high-tech start-up, *MedContrax, Inc.*

Earl earned a Bachelor of Science degree in Electrical Engineering, with honors, from *Tennessee State University*. He graduated from *Arizona State University* with a Master of Science degree in Engineering.

Earl is a former Adjunct Professor of Management at the Keller Graduate School of Management of *DeVry University*. He has completed graduate studies at *Stanford University's Graduate School of Business, the Sloan School of Management at MIT,* and the *Center for Creative Leadership.*

OTHER BOOKS BY
Ervin (Earl) Cobb

The SMART Leader and the Skinny Principles
How to Lead and Win within Any Organization

Driving Ultimate Project Performance
Transforming from Project Manager to Project Leader

The Official Leadership Checklist and Diary for Project Management Professionals

The Leadership Advantage
Do More. Lead More. Earn More.

God's Goodness & Our Mindfulness
Responding versus Reacting to Life Changing Circumstances

Focused Leadership
What You Can Do Today to Become a More Effective Leader

Pillow Talk Consciousness
Intimate Reflections on America's 100 Most Interesting Thoughts and Suspicions

Navigating the Life Enrichment Model™

Living a Richer Life
Getting the Most out of Life's Gifts and Circumstances

www.ingramcontent.com/pod-product-compliance
Lightning Source LLC
LaVergne TN
LVHW051607070426
835507LV00021B/2811